Combing through your SCRAPS

Karen Combs

American Quilter's Society

P. O. Box 3290 • Paducah, KY 42002-3290

e-mail: info@AQSquilt.com

Located in Paducah, Kentucky, the American Quilter's Society (AQS) is dedicated to promoting the accomplishments of today's quilters. Through its publications and events, AQS strives to honor today's quiltmakers and their work and to inspire future creativity and innovation in quiltmaking.

EDITOR: MARJORIE L. RUSSELL
BOOK DESIGN/ILLUSTRATIONS: LYNDA SMITH
COVER DESIGN: MICHAEL BUCKINGHAM
PHOTOGRAPHY: CHARLES R. LYNCH

Library of Congress Cataloging-in-Publication Data
    Combs, Karen.
     Combing through your scraps / by Karen Combs.
       p. cm.
    Includes bibliographical references.
     ISBN 1-57432-761-5
     1. Patchwork--Patterns. 2. Quilting--Patterns. 3. American Quilter's Society. II. Title
     TT835 .C6485 2000
     746.46'041--dc21
                  00-010357

Additional copies of this book may be ordered from the American Quilter's Society, PO Box 3290, Paducah, KY 42002-3290. info@AQSquilt.com

Dedication

To my husband Rick,
daughter Angela,
and son Josh:
Thank you for helping me
turn my passion for quilting
into my dream job!

Acknowledgments

Thank you to all the students who have worked with this method so enthusiastically in workshops and especially to the quilters who sent me photos of their quilts. Most of all, thank you to each quilter who sent work to be photographed for this book: Marilyn Badger, Gail Burrow, Barbara Jo Fish, Gail S. Davis, Beverly Fine, Sue Halsted, Barbie Kanta-Kinsey, Johnnie McCallum, Ruth Spurlock, Nancy Wasserman, and Sheila Woodard.

Thank you to the Pfaff Sewing Machine Company for the loan of the Pfaff 7570. It is a dream to sew and quilt with!

To all the professional and caring people at the American Quilter's Society – it's been a pleasure working with you. Thank you to staff members of both the American Quilter's Society and Collector Books who graciously offered the use of family heirlooms, collections, photos, and even furniture appearing in the photos of the project quilts in this book. My appreciation also to D. J. Lyons of Interiors by D. J. whose artful arrangements of those items enhanced each quilt's design.

Contents

Introduction

I've got to tell you, I love fabric! I've been quilting for more than 20 years and I have more fabric than I can ever use. It doesn't matter, I keep buying more! I wanted to use some of my fabrics to create beautiful scrap quilts. However, I also wanted to make the quilts quickly and have fun doing them. After playing with simple quilt blocks, I came up with this fast and easy method to create scrap quilts using ANY light or dark fabrics.

The ideas in this book are easy. All the quilts can be created using simple Nine-Patch blocks. As you piece a block, you won't have to match colors or patterns in the fabrics. You don't have to agonize over whether "this" red will go with "that" blue. You only look for fabrics that are light or dark. Any color and any pattern can be used. It's a wonderful way to use older fabrics and still make a delightful scrap quilt. Since the blocks and the fabric selection are simple, you can concentrate on the pleasure of sewing.

You will find that these blocks are addictive — it's hard to stop making them. Before you know it, you will have enough blocks to make several wallhangings or a large bed-sized quilt. I've included dozens of patterns and quilt ideas just to keep you going!

Since the quilts in this book are fast and easy, they are perfect to make as gifts. Not only will the person getting the quilt love it, but you will have made a dent in your fabric stash, just in time to buy more fabric!

Enjoy!
Karen

Chapter One
Setting the Stage
Fabric Selection & Preparation

GATHERING FABRICS
So you want to make a scrap quilt; but how do you get started?

Begin your quilt by going through your fabric collection, looking for light fabrics and dark fabrics. Many quilters have a large fabric stash and are anxious to use some of it. Scrap quilts are perfect for using up some of your outdated fabrics. Of course, you can also make a scrap quilt using your favorite fabrics!

Value is the lightness or darkness of a fabric. Since the scrap quilts in this book use only fabrics of light and dark values, the color and the pattern of the fabrics do not matter. Isn't that liberating? You can use fabric you have on hand and make a wonderful quilt, quickly and easily.

You will want a wide variety of colors and patterns, so keep that in mind as you go through your fabric stash. As you spot a light or dark fabric, set it aside. After pulling all the fabrics you think you may want to use, spread them out and look them over. Do you have many different types of light and dark fabrics, or just a few? If you have only a few or all your fabric looks similar, you will need to gather more.

Whether you're a new quilter with a limited fabric stash, or a veteran with a depleted supply, take heart! You can easily gather more fabric. Here are several collection methods:

Ask friends or relatives if they have any whole fabric or fabric scraps they don't want. You will be surprised how many people are happy to give you fabric. Be sure to ask for 100% cotton fabric. It is the fabric quilters prefer to use because it is easy to sew, will not pill, and wears well. As a 100% cotton quilt ages, it develops a wonderful patina that a poly/cotton quilt will never have.

Go to Goodwill or other thrift shops. Many stores have fabrics for sale or old clothes that can be cut up. Check out the remnant tables at fabric stores; they often have a good variety of colors at a low price. Also go to the quilt store and buy fat quarters. This enables you, for a small cost, to buy a wide variety of colors. (Remember – light and dark values only!) Swap pieces with your quilting buddies. For more information on fabric swaps, see Chapter 6.

HOW TO DETERMINE IF YOUR SCRAPS ARE ALL COTTON
Okay, you have lots of scraps, but are they 100% cotton?

It is sometimes hard to tell whether a fabric is 100% cotton or if it is a poly/cotton blend. However, there is an easy way to determine the fiber content of your fabric.

1. Take a small piece of fabric, 2" x 2" or so. Light a match and burn the corner of the fabric. Be careful not to burn yourself! I suggest doing this test over a kitchen sink, so if the flame gets out of hand, you have water handy. If you are checking

many pieces of fabric for fiber content, light a candle, and place it in a holder. Then you can test many pieces without lighting match after match. The fabric may burn quickly, so be ready to blow it out.

2. Once the fabric has cooled, check the burnt edge. Is it soft or crispy? A 100% cotton fabric has a soft edge with a gray ash. A poly/cotton blend will have a crispy feel to its edge. If the poly/cotton blend has a great deal of polyester in it, there may even be a "bead" on the edge from the melted polyester fibers.

FABRIC	EDGE	ASH	SMELL
100% cotton	Soft edge, afterglow	Gray ash	Burning paper
Polyester or Poly Blend	Crispy edge	No ash	Chemical odor

PREPARING NEW FABRIC
Prepare new fabrics using one of several methods.

Read through each description and decide which method best suits your needs. Before doing anything else, first test the fabric for colorfastness. After determining the colorfastness of the fabric, then prewash or preshrink the fabrics, if desired.

Using a light spray sizing on fabrics after washing will add some body to the fabric and make it a delight to cut and sew. Light spray sizing is available at many supermarkets or discount stores. Make sure to purchase light sizing rather than heavy starch since heavy starch makes the fabric too stiff and may flake off as you work with it.

TESTING FABRIC FOR COLORFASTNESS
All fabric should be tested for colorfastness before using.

1. Cut a small piece from each fabric you want to test.

2. Dip each piece in warm water and lay it on a piece of plain white paper towel or bleached muslin.

3. Check to see if any color bleeds onto the paper towel or muslin.

4. If the fabric bleeds, wash the fabric using warm water, but no detergent.

5. After washing, repeat the test.

6. If the fabric still bleeds, it will be necessary to set the dye in the fabric.

SETTING FABRIC DYE
This procedure may prevent fabric dyes from bleeding.

1. Immerse the fabric into undiluted white vinegar. One quart of white vinegar will set approximately 1½ yards of fabric.

2. Leave the fabric in the vinegar for a few minutes then rinse thoroughly in clear, warm water. Repeat the test for colorfastness.

3. If the fabric does not bleed, dry the fabric until slightly damp and iron, using a light spray sizing, if desired.

If the fabric still bleeds after the second test, do not use it in your quilt. Instead, find another fabric to use in its place. Most fabrics do not bleed, but some deep colors such as reds and purples are more likely to cause problems.

You can also use a product called Retayne™. This is a dye fixative that will set commercially dyed fabrics, preventing the fabric from bleeding (see the Sources section, page 86).

PRESHRINKING FABRIC

If your fabric is not dirty, you should use this method to preshrink it before cutting.

1. Sort light and dark fabrics into separate piles. Prepare each pile separately.

2. Unfold fabrics to a single layer.

3. Immerse fabrics in warm, clear water. Do not use detergent.

4. While the fabrics wash, check the water often to see if the water remains clear. If the water is not clear, the fabric is bleeding and will need to be set before using.

5. If the fabric is colorfast, spin the water out using the spin cycle. Place the pieces in a dryer and tumble dry until fabrics are slightly damp. Iron using a light spray sizing.

PREWASHING

This method preshrinks the fabric and removes dirt as well.

However, this method also removes some of the fabric's body. The fabric will be softer and not as crisp as when new.

1. Sort light and dark fabrics into separate piles. Prepare each pile separately.

2. Unfold fabrics to a single layer.

3. Machine wash fabrics in warm water using a mild detergent.

4. Rinse fabrics well and tumble dry. Remove fabrics when slightly damp.

5. Iron using a light spray sizing.

NOT PRESHRINKING OR PREWASHING FABRIC

Some quilters prefer to work with unwashed, new fabric.

Some quilters like the look and feel of new fabric and make their quilts without prewashing or preshrinking. Many never have a problem, especially if they make wallhangings which rarely get dirty and almost never need to be washed. If a wallhanging get dusty, just shake off the dust.

However, if you intend to wash your finished quilt and do not want to prewash, be aware that your fabrics may bleed and could shrink up to approximately three percent. Whether you wash your fabrics or not, testing for colorfastness is always a good idea.

PREPARING OLD FABRIC

Old clothing and used fabrics have already had a chance to shrink, bleed or fade, so they can be washed in a gentler fashion.

However, old clothing is often dirty, so prepare it using the following steps.

1. Cut out all the seams. The fabric is already wear stressed at the seams and it isn't worth the effort to unpick seams.

2. Pick out darts, pleats, and hems.

3. Wash pieces on gentle cycle using warm water and mild detergent. Tumble dry.

4. Press pieces using light spray sizing.

Chapter Two

Now You See It,
Now You Don't

COLOR & VALUE

The scrap quilts presented in this book are a bit different than usual scrap quilts. Usually when selecting fabrics for a quilt, quilters agonize over the colors and the fabrics. "Does this blue go with that red?" "Can a yellow be added to the quilt, or will it overpower the design?" Color can be intimidating for some quilters.

The scrap quilts in this book are a refreshing change. You will find that as you piece these quilts, color does not matter. Strange, isn't it? When you use only five or six colors in a quilt, they must work with each other perfectly. However, when numerous fabrics are used, the color and texture of fabrics do not matter. But, the value is extremely important. In fact, value can make or break your scrap quilt.

These scrap quilts use light and dark fabrics in many different colors and textures. Correct values must be used in these quilts for them to be successful.

WHAT IS VALUE?

Right about now, you may be asking yourself, "I know it's important, but what is value?" Value is the lightness and darkness of a fabric, not how much you paid for it at the store!

In this book, the quilts use only fabrics of light and dark value. Medium value fabrics are used rarely, or not at all.

Many quilters are afraid of value. They don't know whether a fabric is light, medium or dark. It may seem confusing, but doesn't have to be. There are a few tricks and tips that can help determine the value of a fabric.

HOW TO DETERMINE VALUE

Remember, the value of a fabric is its appearance as light or dark. Many times the value of the fabric is relative to neighboring fabrics. This demonstration may help you understand how value is determined.

When this fabric is viewed alone, it appears light in value.

However, when a lighter fabric is placed next to the medium fabric, it looks darker.

When a very dark fabric is laid next to the medium fabric, the medium fabric appears light again.

▲
The medium fabric appears medium when surrounded by a light fabric and a dark fabric.

You can see how a fabric's neighbors can influence its value. But, some fabrics will always be a light or a dark value.

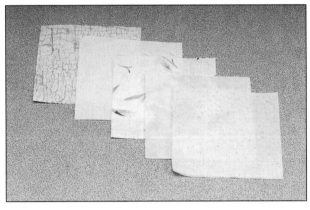

▲
These off-white fabrics are light no matter what fabrics surround them.

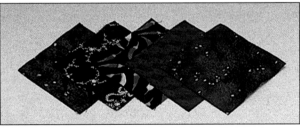

▲
These dark blue fabrics are dark no matter what fabrics surround them.

As you can see, the value of a fabric depends upon the fabric that surrounds it, plus its own lightness or darkness.

VALUE FINDER TOOL

To help determine the value of a fabric, a value finder tool makes the color of the fabric disap-

pear and shows only its lightness or darkness. It is as if the fabric were photocopied in black and white.

There are many types of value finder tools available at quilt shops or from mail order catalogs.

▲
A variety of value finder tools are available at quilt shops or through quilting catalogs.

However, you can easily make a value finder tool from supplies found at an office supply store or discount store.

MAKE VALUE FINDER TOOLS

Purchase two transparent report covers – one red and one green – of the type with a "sliding spine." Make sure the covers are not too dark.

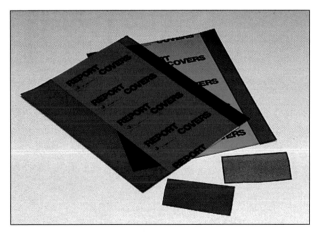

▲
Value finder tools made from supplies found at an office supply store.

Now You See It, Now You Don't

Cut a piece at least 3" x 5" from each cover. Voila! You have just made your own value finder tools. Of course, you can make your pieces larger than 3" x 5" if you wish.

The red value tool will work on all colors of fabric except for red. When determining the value of red fabrics, use the green value tool. Likewise, the green value tool will work on all colors of fabric except for green. So, when determining the value of green fabrics, use the red value tool. Consequently, you will need both red and green value finders as you work with multi-colored fabrics.

For multi-colored fabrics, overlap the tools and use them together. When the value finders are overlapped, the two create a brownish color that will work on almost every color of fabric. You may find using both tools together a bit dark, but you will still be able to see through them.

To use the value finder, select several fabrics whose values are a puzzle. Place them next to, or slightly overlapping, each other. With the tool held close to your eyes, look through it at the fabric. The fabric should appear light or dark, almost black or white, revealing the fabric's value as light or dark.

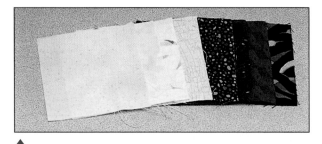
▲
Viewing fabric without the value tools.

▲
Viewing fabric using a red value tool.

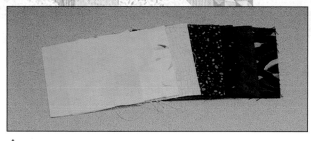
▲
Viewing fabric using a green value tool.

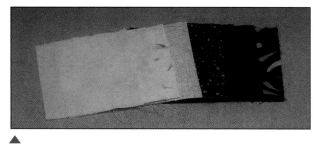
▲
Viewing fabric overlapping the green and red value tools.

Some quilters have trouble using a value tool. Usually it is because they are not using it correctly. A common mistake is to lay the value tool directly on the fabric instead of holding it up to one's eyes. To work correctly, the tool must be held close to one eye and looked through. If you have had trouble with value finders, give this a try.

Basic Scrap Blocks

All of the quilts in this book use a variation of the Nine-Patch Block: Split Nine-Patch, All-Light Nine-Patch, and All-Dark Nine-Patch. By using only these blocks, numerous quilts can be made very quickly and easily. The Split Nine-Patch is the most versatile block of all. Literally dozens of designs can be made using only this block.

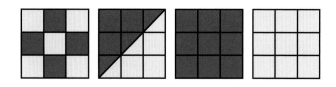
▲
Nine-Patch blocks from left to right: Traditional Nine-Patch, Split Nine-Patch, All-Dark Nine-Patch, All-Light Nine-Patch.

Notice each variation has three rows of three units. The All-Light Nine-Patch is made up of nine light squares. The All-Dark Nine-Patch is made up of nine dark squares.

A Split Nine-Patch block is divided into two sides. One side is dark and the other side is light. This block uses squares and half-square triangles.

USING DIFFERENT PRINTS AND COLORS

These blocks are fun and easy to piece. Any color or texture of fabric will work. Don't worry about matching colors. In these blocks, value is the only concern. Isn't that a nice change of pace?

Before piecing a block, begin by laying out the shapes for several blocks. Then you can see how a finished block will look.

▲
Example of an All-Light Nine-Patch block.

▲
Example of an All-Dark Nine-Patch block.

At first, you may think all the different colors and textures look funny together, but as long as they have compatible values, the block will be

correct. When blocks are used in a design, it is difficult to identify the individual colors or textures. Only the overall design is seen.

When laying out a Split Nine-Patch, take a look at the block and ask yourself if you can see a line between the light and dark sides. If you see a distinct line, the values are correct. If the two sides blend together, the values are too close and will need to be corrected.

▲
Example of a balanced Split Nine-Patch block.

Also, if a patch is too dark, try turning it over. Fabric is often lighter on the back (or wrong) side of the fabric and using it may be an option when sewing the block.

▲
Split Nine-Patch block without distinct light and dark values.

When laying out the All-Light or All-Dark Nine-Patches, take some time to make certain the blocks look all light or all dark. Time spent now will ensure that values are correct in the finished blocks.

Chapter Three
Quiltmaking Magic
Cutting, Piecing, Pressing & Quilting

ROTARY CUTTERS

Rotary cutters have made quiltmaking faster and very accurate. Using a rotary cutter, it is possible to cut many layers of fabric at one time. Even squares and triangles emerge with lightning speed!

A rotary cutter resembles a pizza cutter, but is much sharper. The cutter has a built-in guard to shield the sharp blade when not in use. For safety's sake, always close the guard when the cutter is not in use. Remember to stand when rotary cutting. Standing provides a better view and more control over the ruler and cutter.

Reserve a rotary cutter exclusively to cut fabrics. Switch blades if you want to cut paper or plastic with your rotary cutter since those materials quickly dull the rotary blade. Many quilters have a "paper and plastic" rotary cutter and a "fabric" rotary cutter.

Dull and worn rotary cutter blades skip along the fabric instead of cutting smoothly and cleanly. Carefully clean or replace blades as soon as they begin to show wear.

SAFETY TIPS
- Make sure to close the guard whenever the rotary cutter is not in use.
- Keep fingers away from the open blade.
- Keep rotary cutters out of reach of children.
- Cut away from yourself, never toward you.

MATS

Use a self-healing cutting mat with your rotary cutter. It not only protects the work surface from the sharp blade but also makes the blade last longer. Without a cutting mat, you will find the blade dulls almost at once.

If you have a large cutting area, the large 24" x 36" mat is a good size to have. But, if your cutting area is limited, you might consider the 18" x 24" mat, the size most quilters use.

Be sure to store your cutting mat flat; do not fold it. Keep it away from direct sunlight and heat since they can warp the mat. If you have room, keep your mat in your sewing room, flat on a table. That way, you will always have a handy cutting surface.

Many quilters don't have the luxury of a sewing room and must store their quilting supplies when not in use. There are several ways to store a cutting mat — flat, against a wall, or even hidden behind a sofa or a bookcase.

Here's another option. A skirt hanger with soft protectors on the clips will prevent the clips from scratching the mat's soft surface. Clip the mat to the hanger and hang it in a closet or on the back of a door.

RULERS

Many types of rulers can be used with rotary cutters. The most useful rulers are made of heavy, clear plastic or acrylic and are $\frac{1}{8}$" thick with straight, smooth edges. Many quilters favor 6" x 24" or 6" x 12" rulers to cut strips and 6" x 6" rulers to cut squares and triangles.

There are rulers with yellow markings, black markings, and even pink markings. Try out different brands to see which works best for you.

ROTARY CUTTING STRIPS

Cotton fabrics vary in width. When purchasing fabric, assume the width of the fabric is 42", no matter what it says on the end of the bolt!

Fabrics are cut on the crosswise grain from selvage to selvage. The instructions in this book are for right-handed quilters. If you are left-handed, reverse the instructions and use a ruler with markings for both right-handed and left-handed quilters.

1. Place a piece of fabric on your cutting mat and fold it in half with the fold of the fabric toward you. Make sure the fabric is not wrinkled. If your rotary blade is sharp, you can stack up to three or four fabrics, which will give you six to eight layers.

    The fold of the top fabric should be ¼" or so above the fold of the fabric below. This ensures that your strips will be cut at 90 degrees to the fold.

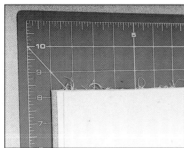

Stacked fabrics, ready to rotary cut.

2. Align the bottom fabric with a horizontal line on your cutting mat. Move the left vertical edge of the fabric until it is slightly over a vertical line on your cutting mat.

3. Trim the edge of the fabric by placing the 6" x 12" or 6" x 24" rotary ruler on the vertical line on the cutting mat.

Line up the ruler with the vertical line on the mat.

Place the weight of your left hand on the ruler, keeping one finger along the left edge of the ruler to prevent it from slipping. With your right hand, remove the cutter guard and hold the cutter straight, with the blade snug against the right edge of the ruler.

Press down firmly on the cutter and push it away from you in a smooth, strong motion, maintaining a uniform pressure. Remember to keep the blade tight against the ruler and avoid short, jerky cuts.

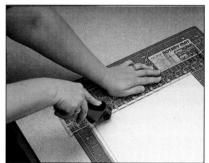

Push the cutter away from you in a smooth, strong motion.

The uneven edge of the fabric is trimmed off.

4. Remove and discard the trimmed edges of fabric. Slide the ruler to the right until the markings on the ruler are at the desired strip width. If you want to cut 3½" strips, align the left edge of your fabric exactly with the 3½" marking on the ruler.

As described above, roll the cutter against the right edge of the ruler, maintaining an even pressure.

◄ Align the ruler with the desired strip width and cut against the right edge of the ruler.

5. Cut as many strips in your desired size as needed. Replace the guard on the rotary cutter before setting it down.

CUTTING SHAPES FROM STRIPS

Several shapes are needed to make any of the basic Nine-Patch blocks — the All-Light Nine-Patch, All-Dark Nine-Patch, and Split Nine-Patch. For these blocks, squares and/or half-square triangles are required. A half-square triangle is a square made from two triangles of different fabrics. When sewn together along their longest sides and pressed, they form a square.

▲ Square and half-square triangle.

Many patterns in this book use a 3" finished size for the squares and triangles. Check pattern instructions before cutting the shapes.

SQUARES

To rotary cut 3" squares, cut a strip 3½" x 42", or the width of the fabric.

Lay the strip on the cutting mat and position a 6" x 6" ruler on the strip. If needed, trim off the left edge. Before each cut, position the ruler with the 3½" marking even with the left edge of the fabric. Each sewn square will measure 3".

▲ Cut squares from a precut strip.

3½" squares: (42" wide fabric)
one yard – yields 120 ½ yard – yields 60 ¼ yard – yields 24

FABRIC YIELD FOR SQUARES

Yardage listings are based on 42" fabric width. Preshrink or allow for up to 3 percent shrinkage and trimming of selvages.

When using different sized squares or triangles, refer to the charts for fabric yield.

Finished size	(cut)	1 yard	½ yard	¼ yard
1½"	(2")	378	189	84
2"	(2½")	224	112	48
2½"	(3")	168	84	42
3"	(3½")	120	60	24
3½"	(4")	90	40	20
4"	(4½")	72	36	18

HALF-SQUARE TRIANGLES

To rotary cut 3" half-square triangles, cut a strip of fabric 3⅞" by 42", or the width of your fabric. Lay the strip on the cutting mat and position a 6" x 6" ruler on the strip. If needed, trim off the left edge. Before cutting, position the ruler with the 3⅞" marking even with the left edge of the fabric. Cut squares and then cut those squares diagonally from corner to corner. After sewing a light and dark triangle together, the finished square will measure 3".

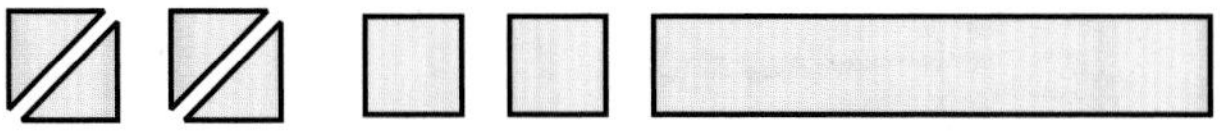

To make half-square triangles, cut strips in the desired width, cut squares and then cut the squares from corner to corner.

3⅞" squares, cut into triangles:
one yard = 90 squares/180 triangles
½ yard = 40 squares/80 triangles
¼ yard = 20 squares/40 triangles

FABRIC YIELD FOR TRIANGLES

Yardage listings are based on 42" fabric width. Preshrink or allow for up to 3 percent shrinkage and trimming of selvages.

When using different sized squares or triangles, refer to the charts for fabric yield.

Finished size	(cut)	1 yard	½ yard	¼ yard
1½"	(2⅜")	510	238	102
2"	(2⅞")	336	168	84
2½"	(3⅜")	240	120	48
3"	(3⅞")	180	80	40
3½"	(4⅜")	144	72	36
4"	(4⅞")	112	48	16

TEMPLATES

Many quilters prefer to use templates rather than rotary cutting their shapes. To use templates, follow the next steps.

MAKING TEMPLATES

1. Place tracing paper over the desired template pattern. Using a ruler and a pencil, trace sewing and cutting lines, grainlines, and size markings. Using paper scissors, cut out the tracing paper a bit larger than needed.

After tracing markings, cut out tracing paper a bit larger than needed.

2. Smear glue stick onto template plastic and place the paper template onto the glue. Smooth out any air bubbles and apply more glue to the edges of the template, if needed.

3. Using paper scissors, cut out the template directly on the cutting line.

CUTTING FABRIC USING TEMPLATES

1. With the wrong side up, place a single layer of fabric on cutting board.

2. Place the template on fabric, aligning the grainline on the template to the lengthwise grain of the fabric.

3. Using a sharp lead pencil, trace around template. You can use a silver, white or yellow pencil if you wish. Trace around as many shapes as you need, marking only half the width of the fabric.

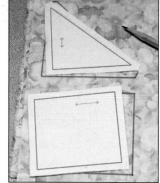

◄ Trace around templates, using a sharp pencil.

4. Fold the fabric in half, with template markings face up. Place a pin in the middle of each template. Make sure the fabric is not wrinkled. With sharp scissors, it is possible to cut up to two or three fabrics (four to six layers).

5. Cut out the shapes. When cutting many layers, hold scissors perpendicular to the fabric to ensure an accurate cut of all layers.

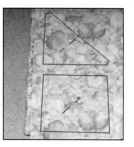

► Fold fabric in half, pin the center of each template, cut shapes on pencil line.

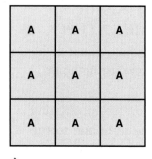 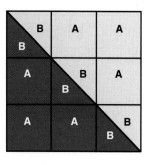

▲ Template placement guide for Nine-Patch and Split Nine-Patch blocks.

SORTING THE VALUES

After cutting the shapes, sort them into light and dark values. Be sure to read Chapter 2, "Now You See It, Now You Don't," before sorting your fabrics.

Sort into the following piles: light triangles, dark triangles, light squares, and dark squares. Don't mix sizes! Keep all 3½" squares together, all 3⅞" triangles together, etc. After sorting, it is a good idea to place each shape and value into its own shallow box for storage. Shirt gift boxes make excellent storage places. The boxes can be labeled and are easily stored.

HAND PIECING

Most quilters prefer to machine piece, however, some might prefer hand piecing. Hand piecing gives a soft edge to seams and is done using a small, even running stitch. Hand piecing offers the advantage of allowing you to take your sewing with you.

1. Mark the ¼" stitching line on the wrong side of every fabric piece using a small ruler and a pencil.

2. Cut an 18" length of neutral-colored thread, knot one end, and thread it through a #10 between quilting needle. (It may help to use a needle threader.) Hand piecing stitches are made with a single strand of thread.

3. Place two shapes with right sides together and pin the corners. Sew from one corner to the other with a small running stitch, keeping the tension even. Tie off with a knot. Some quilters prefer not to use knots and instead, take a few backstitches at the beginning and the end of each seam.

4. Hand piecing allows greater control when fitting shapes together. Shapes can be matched perfectly at the intersections. Match seams as described for machine piecing. Do not sew into the seam allowances when sewing rows together. Stitch only on the lines. When needed, flip back the seam allowance and continue sewing.

MACHINE PIECING
SEAM ALLOWANCES

Machine piecing is a fast and easy way to make scrap quilts, the method most quilters prefer. When machine piecing, use an accurate ¼" (.75 cm) seam allowance. The seam allowance is the distance from the cut edge of the fabric to the stitching line.

Before starting to machine piece, check your sewing machine's seam allowance guide. If you have been using the right edge of your presser foot as a guide, you may be surprised to find that your seam allowance is not ¼".

If you find your seam allowance is not ¼", there are several ways to ensure accuracy.

The needle position on many machines can be adjusted to allow for an accurate ¼" seam allowance while using the edge of the presser foot as a guide. Check your sewing machine manual if you are unsure whether or not your sewing machine has adjustable needle positions.

To use the adjustable needle feature, with the presser foot up, place the ¼" line on a ruler next to the edge of your presser foot. Move your needle to the edge of your ruler.

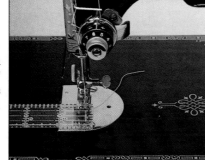

Checking for an accurate ¼" seam allowance using a ruler.

If you cannot adjust the needle position on your sewing machine, check with a sewing machine dealer to see if a ¼" presser foot is available for your sewing machine. Quilt shops and mail order catalogs also offer presser feet.

If you can't adjust your needle or find a ¼" presser foot, make a ¼" mark on your machine's throat plate. To do this, draw a line on a small piece of plain paper, using a ruler and sharp pencil. Move the ruler over to the right ¼" and draw a second line. Cut the paper exactly on the second line. You can also simplify the process by using the lines on ¼" graph paper.

Insert the paper under the needle, lower the presser foot onto the first line, and stitch without thread for several inches. With the paper still in place and the presser foot and needle down, position a piece of thin masking tape along the edge of the paper. Remove the paper and use the edge of the tape as a seam gauge.

Checking ¼" seam allowance with paper.

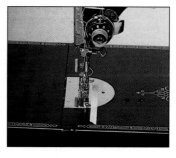

When the paper is removed, the tape will provide an accurate ¼" seam allowance guide.

NEEDLES AND THREAD

Leading needle manufacturers recommend starting every new sewing project with a new needle. However, since piecing a quilt takes longer than most sewing projects, change your needle after every eight to ten hours of sewing.

Listen closely as you sew, and with practice, you will be able to tell when the needle needs to be changed. The sound of the needle entering the fabric will change from a smooth, gliding sound to a slight "popping" sound as the needle wears. However, even if you don't hear a sound difference, it's still a good idea to change needles frequently and to use good quality needles. A burred needle can run fabric, and cheap needles often break easily.

Sewing machine needles come in many different types and sizes. The type of needle you should use depends upon the weight of your fabric and the type of sewing you are doing. Needles are sized by a numbering system; the lower the number, the finer the needle.

Generally, when machine piecing, a #12/80 universal needle is a good size to use. That needle has a slight ball point shape and is used for most general sewing on woven fabrics.

However, many quilters prefer to use a #10/75 jeans needle for machine piecing. It is a finer, sharper needle and leaves a smaller hole in the fabric. Experiment with needles to see which you prefer.

To avoid puckering, use a fine, sharp needle and a straight stitch throat plate. Often an optional accessory for your machine, a straight stitch throat plate has a round hole for the needle as opposed to the wide hole designed for zigzag sewing. Using a jeans needle with a straight stitch throat plate will yield an even, beautiful seam. Remember to change back to the zigzag throat plate when you are finished machine piecing or you'll break your needle the first time you zigzag!

Along with a straight stitch throat plate, a straight stitch presser foot is recommended. Like the throat plate, it has a small round hole instead of a wide rectangular one.

Use cotton or cotton covered polyester thread. Do not use quilting thread. Quilting thread is for hand quilting, not machine piecing. Don't try to save money by buying cheap thread from the bargain bin. It breaks easily and in the long run, is not a bargain. Buy a good quality thread. You will be glad you did.

Use a neutral thread color, such as off-white, beige, or even a light gray. Using a neutral thread color means it won't be necessary to change thread to match the fabric for every seam. Neutral thread works with every color fabric, even dark fabrics. For best results, use the same type of thread for both upper and bobbin threading in your sewing machine.

To save time while sewing, wind several bobbins ahead of time. When you run out of bobbin thread, just pop in a prewound bobbin rather than taking the time to rewind.

For American-made sewing machines, set your machine at 10–12 stitches per inch, a good straight stitch setting for machine piecing.

European machines use a different numbering system. Stitch lengths are set from .5 to 4 mm. Set your machine at 2 or 2.5 mm for machine piecing.

CHAIN PIECING

Chain piecing saves time and thread. To chain piece, align the edge of two patches, and sew them. Then, without stopping to clip the thread, lift the presser foot, slip the next two aligned pieces under the toes of the presser foot. This is called chain piecing because there will be a little chain of thread between the patches. Cut the chain after sewing a few patches. Don't worry about backstitching. Since seams will cross each other, the stitching will be secure.

Chain piece to save time and thread.

SEWING ROWS AND INTERLOCKING SEAMS

Proper pinning is the key to sewing accurate rows and interlocking seams. There is a right and a wrong way to use pins. Pin perpendicular to the seam and never sew over pins. Slip pins out of the fabric just as they move under the presser foot. Pin only when necessary to match seams or to sew long seams.

SQUARES

Line up the matching seams and slide them together. The seams should interlock, forming a tight match. Pin on either side of the seam. Remember to remove the pins as you sew. Don't sew over them!

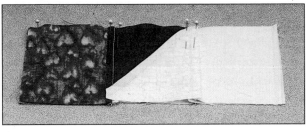

▲
Line up seams and pin on either side of the seam.

TRIANGLES

Stick a pin in the center of the triangle and line it up with the square below. Hold the pieces tightly together and pin on either side of the first pin, then remove the middle pin.

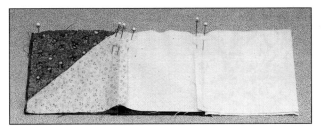

▲
Line up seams and pin on either side of the seam.

Stitch up to the pins and remove them when the sewing machine needle is in the down position right next to the pin. Stitching will go through the intersection of the seam.

SPEED BLOCK ASSEMBLY
Split Nine-Patch

Before sewing, check for an accurate ¼" seam allowance. Lay out a block and using the value tool, double-check the block, making sure the block has a light side and a dark side.

◀
Laying out a Split Nine-Patch block.

1. Sew each pair of triangles together. Clip threads between triangles and press. Trim off fabric "tails" and place pairs back into position in the block.

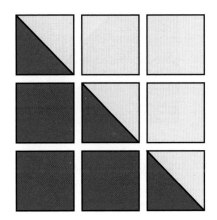

2. Sew patches together. Press seams and place back into position.

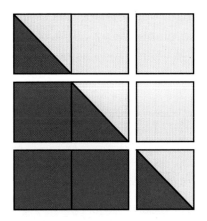

3. Sew remaining patches together and press seams. Place the patch back into position and you should have three rows.

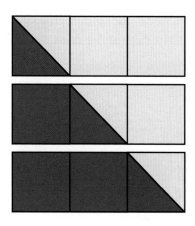

4. Match seams, pin and sew rows together.

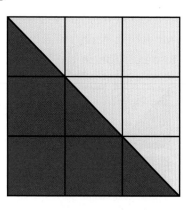

5. After the block is sewn, measure it. If it is too big or too small, check your seam allowance measurement and resew.

ALL-DARK AND ALL-LIGHT BLOCKS

The all-light and all-dark blocks are pieced in the same manner. Lay out a block and chain piece it, matching rows as needed.

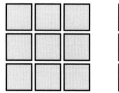

▲
Piecing an All-Light Nine-Patch block.

PRESSING TIPS AND OPTIONS

It is important to press seams while sewing. Pressing helps match the seams and ensures the finished block will be the correct size. Keep your ironing board close to the machine. Or, if you like the exercise, place the board across the room so you are forced to get up and move!

Use a well-padded pressing surface or ironing board. A thick, light-colored towel placed next to your sewing machine also makes a good pressing surface. The towel prevents seam allowances from creating a ridge on the right side of your pieces.

Pressing is not ironing! Pressing is an up-and-down motion, while ironing involves pushing the iron. Ironing can distort the block and stretch the pieces out of shape. To press correctly, set the iron down on the seam, apply momentary pressure, steam if desired, lift the iron straight up, and move to another spot.

After sewing a seam, there are several pressing options. Whichever method you use, first press the wrong side of the fabric. Then give the front of the seam a good press.

The fastest and simplest way to press is to press seams toward the darker color. This is a traditional method for pressing seams.

▶
Press seam allowances toward the dark fabric.

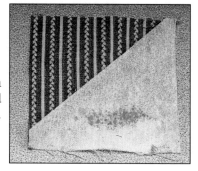

The seams are strong and don't allow the batting to beard along the seam lines. Pressing toward the dark also prevents shadowing of the seam. Shadowing is when the seam allowance is seen through a light fabric.

To press toward the dark, use the edge of the iron to push the seams toward the darker fabric with most of the iron's weight off the ironing surface. After the seam is pushed toward the dark, rest the weight of the iron on the seam, give the seam a bit of steam if desired, and lift the iron. Repeat on the next seam.

Pressing seams open is a fairly new and controversial method requiring more time and effort. The results are worth it since open seams produce a smooth quilt top that lays flat and hangs straight. It makes matching points a snap.

If you use open seams, do not quilt using a stitch-in-the-ditch quilting stitch. Stitching along the pressed open seam breaks the piecing thread. Use stitch-in-the-ditch quilting only on seams that are pressed toward the dark or to one side.

To press open, sew the pieces together, smoothing the seams open with your fingers or with the tip of an iron. Rest the weight of the iron on the open seam and give it a bit of steam, if desired. Lift the iron straight up and repeat on the next seam.

QUILTING OPTIONS

Many quilting options are available when quilting a scrap quilt. Hand quilting is one option; however, with the numerous seams, it will be difficult to hand piece through all the seams. You may prefer to machine quilt your scrap quilt.

Machine quilting is a fast and easy way to finish a scrap quilt. Quilting options include outline quilting, stitching in the ditch or freehand quilting.

Wallhangings can be either heavily quilted or lightly quilted. For a stiffer wallhanging, heavily quilt it using stipple freehand quilting.

Bed quilts need to drape easily across a bed. For a softer, more drapeable quilt, quilt it lightly using parallel stitching in the ditch.

For more design ideas, refer to Chapter 5, "Magic Results From Simple Blocks." Quilting diagrams for each quilt are found in the pattern section.

◀ Open seams with the tip of the iron.

▶ Seams pressed open.

TEMPLATES

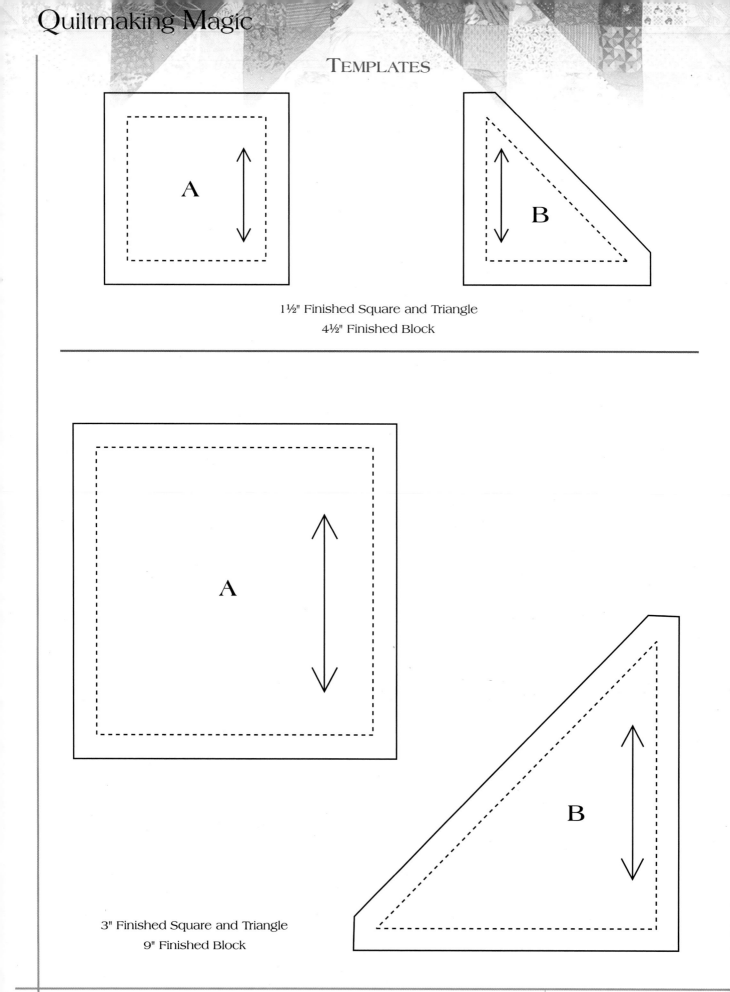

A

B

1½" Finished Square and Triangle
4½" Finished Block

A

B

3" Finished Square and Triangle
9" Finished Block

TEMPLATES

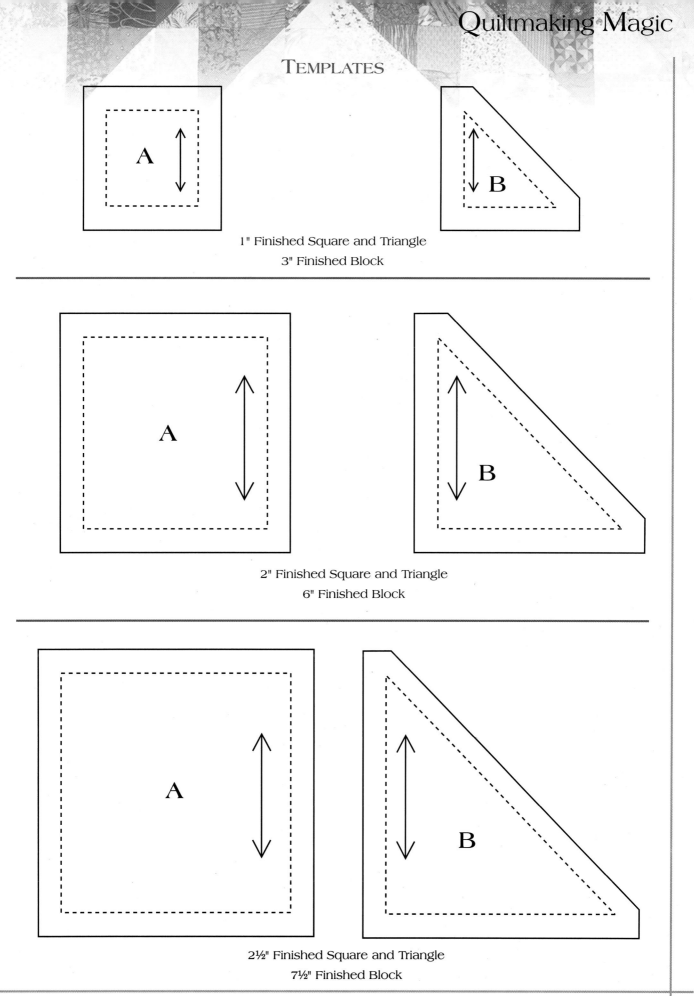

1" Finished Square and Triangle
3" Finished Block

2" Finished Square and Triangle
6" Finished Block

2½" Finished Square and Triangle
7½" Finished Block

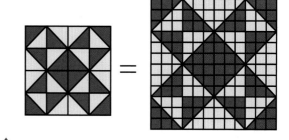

Chapter Four
Design Sleight of Hand

BLOCKS, DESIGNS, AND SIZES

The blocks — Split Nine-Patch, All-Light Nine-Patch and All-Dark Nine-Patch — are simple, easy-to-piece quilt blocks. It may be hard to believe these humble blocks can create interesting quilt designs, but don't let them fool you. When the blocks are set together, a vast variety of quilt designs is possible. In fact, you will be amazed at the hundreds of designs that are possible using just these three blocks.

To help you discover the design possibilities, look at a quilt block encyclopedia for quilt blocks that use ONLY half-square triangles, light squares, and dark squares. There are numerous quilt blocks using only these shapes. In fact, many quilt blocks, such as Variable Star, use only half-square triangles.

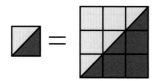

Half-square triangle patch = Split Nine-Patch

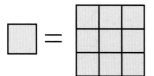

Light square patch = All-Light Nine-Patch

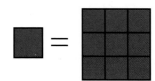

Dark square patch = All-Dark Nine-Patch

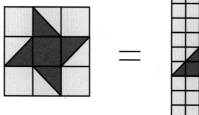

▲
A Variable Star quilt block turns into a Variable Star scrap wallhanging.

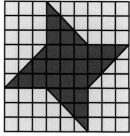

▲
A Friendship Star quilt blocks turns into a Friendship Star scrap wallhanging.

While looking at different quilt blocks, notice how the shapes, the half-square triangles, and the squares correspond to the Nine-Patch blocks. Using this knowledge, you can turn many different traditional quilt blocks into wonderful scrap quilts!

Pieced quilt blocks are actually grids, divided into sections. Grids are identified by the number of times they are divided into equal parts. For example, a simple Nine-Patch block could also be correctly identified as a Nine-Patch grid.

When designing a quilt, the possibilities are endless if you think in terms of using a favorite block pattern, but expanding it into a larger grid.

FOUR-PATCH GRID

Four-Patch grids are quilt blocks that have been divided into four equal parts.

The following 16-square Four-Patch quilt blocks make wonderful scrap quilt wallhangings or throws.

▲ Four-Patch grid. This can be further divided into a 16-square Four Patch.

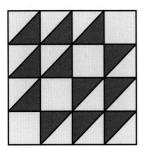

▲ A 16-square Four-Patch grid.

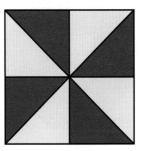

▲ Sugar Bowl.

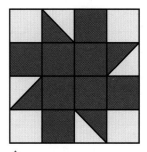

▲ Friendship Four-Patch.

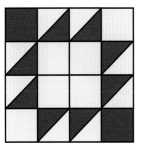

▲ Marching to Zion.

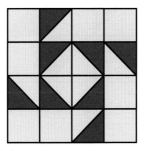

▲ Skip to My Lou.

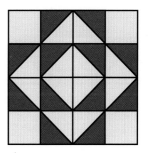

▲ Garden Glade.

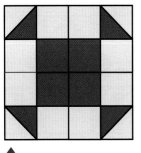

▲ Bond of Love.

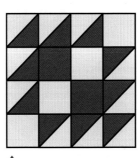

▲ Star Wreath.

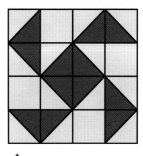

▲ Next Door Neighbor.

Design Sleight of Hand

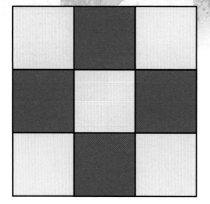

▲ A Nine-Patch grid.

NINE-PATCH GRID

Nine-Patch grids are quilt blocks that have been divided into three equal parts.

The following Nine-Patch quilt blocks will make delightful small quilts for use as wallhangings, table toppers or baby quilts.

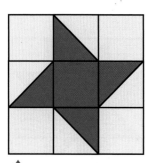

▲
Friendship Star.

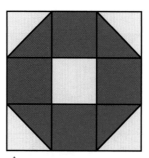

▲
Single Wedding Ring.

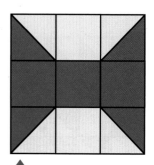

▲
Bow Tie.

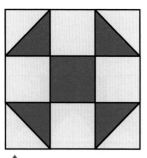

▲
Shoo Fly.

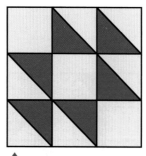

▲
Double X.

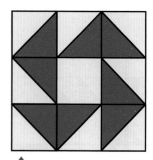

▲
Ribbons.

The Nine-Patch grid can also be divided further, into a 6 x 6 grid. These quilt blocks use a 36-square Nine-Patch grid and work well as scrap quilts. They will be larger than the previous quilts, so they work well as throws or large wallhangings.

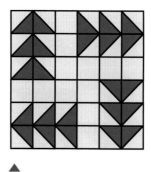

▲
36-square Nine-Patch grid.

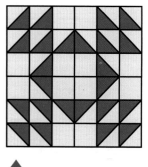

▲
Flying Geese.

▲
Nine-Patch Variation.

FIVE-PATCH GRID

A Five-Patch grid is a square that has been divided into five equal parts. It has five rows by five rows or 25 squares.

These quilt blocks make wonderful large wallhangings or throws.

▲ A Five-Patch grid.

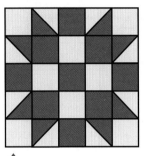

▲ Sister's Choice.

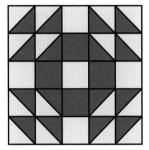

▲ Wedding Ring.

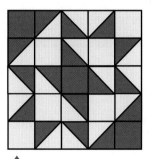

▲ Queen Charlotte's Crown.

REALISTIC QUILT BLOCKS

A realistic quilt block is one that contains a pictorial representation rather than a geometric design. These quilt blocks can become delightful wallhangings or baby quilts.

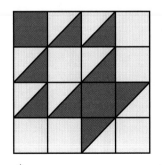

▲ Basket Quilt.

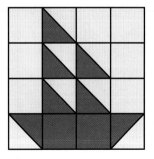

▲ Fishing Boats.

Design Sleight of Hand

TRADITIONAL LOG CABIN SETTING

Another source of inspiration for scrappy quilts is traditional Log Cabin settings. As you know, Log Cabin blocks have a dark side and a light side, making them perfect additions to scrappy quilts using Split Nine-Patch blocks.

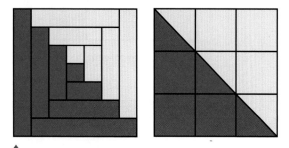

▲
A Log Cabin quilt block has a light and dark side as does the Split Nine-Patch block.

Log Cabin settings offer several options. Use a few blocks, perhaps 16, to make a wallhanging or a baby quilt. More blocks create a bed-sized quilt. If you want to make a bed-sized quilt, the chart on page 35 will help you determine what size quilt to make.

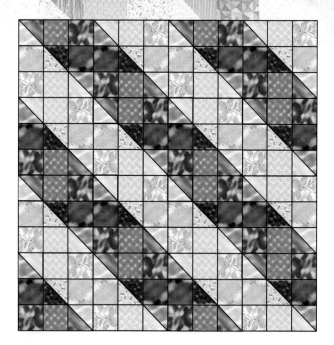

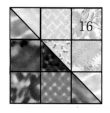

▲
Straight Furrows setting using 16 Split Nine-Patch blocks.

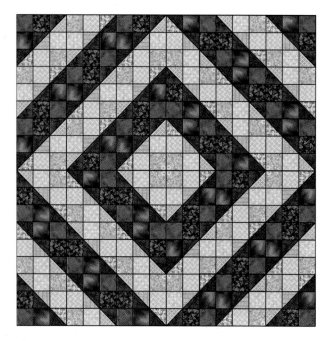

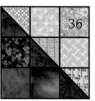

▲
Barn Raising setting using 36 split Nine-Patch blocks.

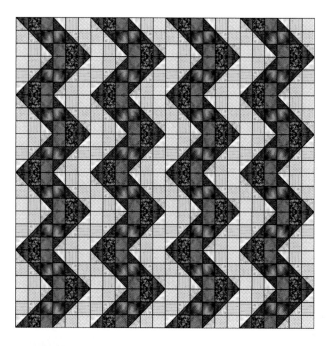

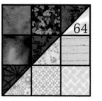

▲
A scrap quilt in a Streak of Lightning setting using 64 Split Nine-Patch blocks.

Triangles from Squares

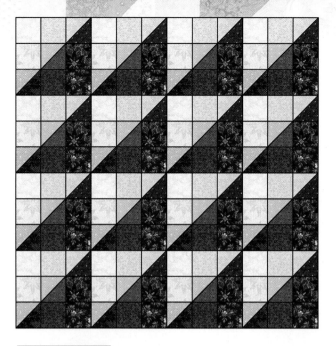

This Sunshine and Shadow setting uses 16 Split Nine-Patch blocks.

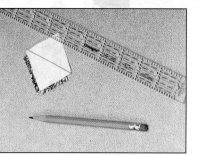

▶ Place a light and a dark square with right sides together. Using a pencil and ruler, draw a line from corner to corner.

◀ Sew on the line.

▶ Cut ¼" from sewn line. Press the seam to one side and trim off the excess.

◀ Voila! A 2" triangle unit from 2" squares!

Miniature Scrap Quilts Using Watercolor Squares

Many quilters have made watercolor quilts. This popular technique uses squares that are cut 2". To get good variety in watercolor quilts, quilters cut hundreds of different squares with the result that many now have boxes and boxes of leftover squares. These 2" squares are perfect for making miniature scrap quilts.

The Split Nine-Patch block uses both squares and triangles but you may have only 2" watercolor squares. Don't worry, you don't have to cut extra 2" triangles. There is a quick trick that can be used to create triangles from 2" squares.

Use your 2" watercolor squares to create wonderful miniature quilts. Any design in this book can be used to create a scrap quilt with 2" squares. It will be a smaller quilt, but it will be just as lovely as a larger quilt!

Design Sleight of Hand

You can make dozens, even hundreds, of designs using only light and dark Nine-Patch and Split Nine-Patch blocks. Twist and turn blocks on a design wall or use computer software developed for quilters.

Keep working at it and you'll be amazed at the results. Here are just a few of the design possibilities. The numbers in the blocks below the design show how many blocks you need to make the design.

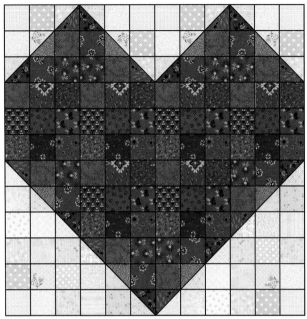

▲ A sweet, scrappy heart, perfect for a baby.

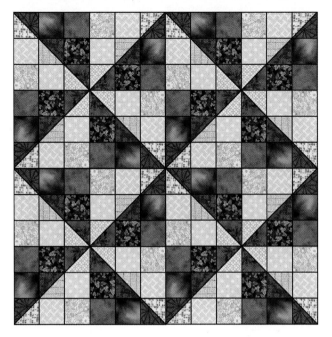

▲ By itself, the traditional block, Pinwheel, is a simple design. Look what happens when several are set next to each other!

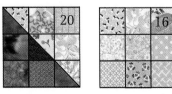

▲ Pinwheels and All-Light Nine-Patches make a delightful design.

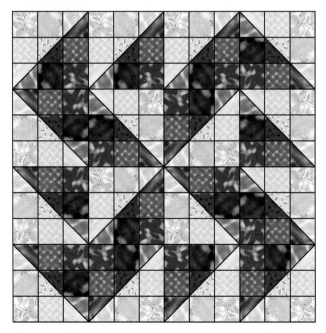

▲ The traditional Dutchman's Puzzle quilt block inspired this setting.

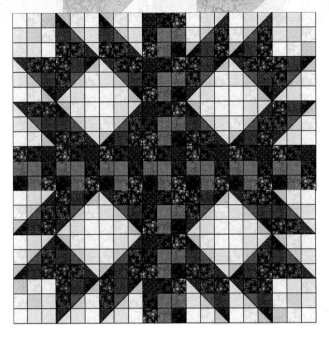

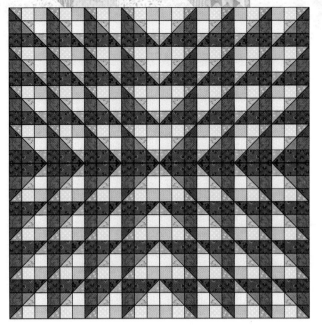

▲ In this Bear's Paw quilt, the "paws" have a light on-point square in them.

▲ The traditional Flying Geese quilt block inspired this setting.

 32  13 4

64

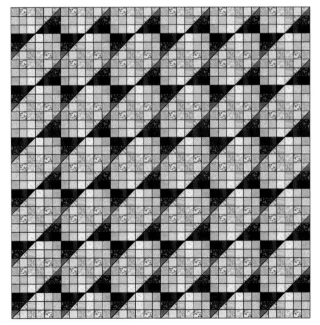

▲ Light and dark Flying Geese blocks surround the center of this quilt. The result is an absorbing quilt design.

▲ It's surprising to realize this beautiful quilt design is made from just two simple quilt blocks.

64

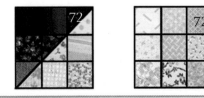 72 72

Design Sleight of Hand

▲ A repeating pattern of star points produces a delightful design.

▲ An engaging setting combines a center star with diamonds along the border of the quilt.

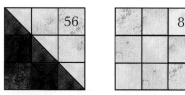

▲ A star surrounded by a striking dark border creates a pleasant design.

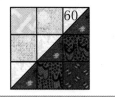

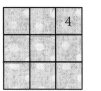

▲ Stars and multiple borders produce a delightful quilt.

DESIGNING YOUR OWN

You can also design your own quilts using Split Nine-Patch, All-Light Nine-Patch, and All-Dark Nine-Patch blocks. Create your own designs by playing with the blocks until you find a pleasing design. You will be surprised by what you create!

WHAT SIZE SHOULD I MAKE MY QUILT?

Wallhangings, throws, baby quilts or table toppers can be just about any size. However, if you are making a quilt for a particular bed, it is important that the quilt fit the bed. If you are not sure how to go about making a quilt for a certain bed, the information in this section will help.

DETERMINING YOUR IDEAL QUILT SIZE

Making a bed quilt begins with determining the ideal finished size. When making a quilt for a particular bed, measure the length and the width of the mattress. If the bed is unavailable for measure, the length and width measurements of standard mattresses are listed below.

Standard Mattress Sizes*

Crib: 27" x 52"

Twin: 39" x 75"

Full: 54" x 75"

Queen: 60" x 80"

King: 72" x 84"

*No "drop" has been added.

After measuring the top of the mattress, add the drop. The drop is the distance the quilt falls from the top edge of the mattress toward the floor. The amount of drop to add is up to you, but keep in mind that your quilt will need to cover bed linens beneath the quilt. Add drop measurements equally to both sides and the foot of the bed.

If pillow shams will be used, there is no need to add a drop to the head of the bed. For a quilt that covers pillows, add an additional 12" to 18" to the length of the quilt.

With the addition of quilting stitches, a quilt can draw up, typically becoming about an inch smaller all around after quilting. A quilt that is heavily quilted may be even smaller. Keep this in mind while planning your quilt.

Use this chart to determine finished quilt size:

	Width	Length
Mattress dimensions:	_____" x	_____"
Add drop Right side	_____"	
Left side	_____"	
Bottom		_____"
Add to cover pillows		_____"
Add to compensate for quilting "draw up"	_____"	_____"
	_____"	_____"
Total	_____" x	_____"

CHOOSING A BLOCK SIZE

Once you have calculated the finished quilt size, then determine your block size. Since these quilts are made from scraps, check your scrap-bag first to see what size squares and triangles you already have. If you have many squares and triangles of a certain size, consider using them. An inventory of the fabric shapes you already have may influence your decision on block size.

Many quilting projects use 3½" squares and triangles. Because of that, many quilters have extras of this size in their scrap bags. With that in mind, many of the patterns in this book are based on 3" finished squares and triangles.

Design Sleight of Hand

The size of squares and triangles determines the size of the block. Use small squares or triangles and the finished block will be smaller. Smaller blocks mean that more blocks will be needed to make the quilt.

If your squares and triangles are larger, your finished blocks will be larger and fewer blocks will be needed for your quilt. The chart below will help determine the finished size of the block.

The term "unfinished" refers to the size of the block with seam allowances before it is sewn into the quilt. The term "finished" refers to the size of the block after it is sewn into the quilt.

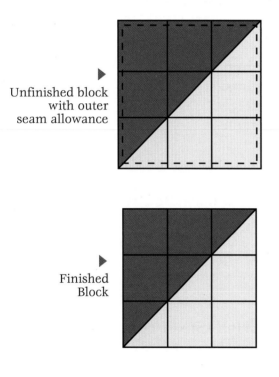

▶ Unfinished block with outer seam allowance

▶ Finished Block

Cut squares	Cut triangles	Unfinished block size	Finished block size
1½"	1⅞"	3½"	3"
2"	2⅜"	5"	4½"
2½"	2⅞"	6½"	6"
3"	3⅜"	8"	7½"
3½	3⅞"	9½"	9"
4"	4⅜"	11"	10½"

HOW MANY BLOCKS WILL YOU NEED?

Now that you know the size of your finished quilt and the size of your blocks, it's time to determine how many blocks you will need.

To find the number of blocks needed for your quilt, divide the size of your finished block size into first the width of the finished quilt, and then the length. This will give the number of blocks across and down the quilt.

Example:

Quilt size: 72" x 90"
Finished block size: 9"

$$72" \div 9" = 8$$
$$90" \div 10" = 9$$

In this case, the quilt is 8 blocks wide by 9 blocks long for a total of 72 blocks.

But what happens if your division does not yield a whole number?

Example:

Quilt size: 72" x 90"
Finished block size: 12"

$$72" \div 12" = 6$$
$$90" \div 12" = 7.5$$

In this case, the quilt is 6 blocks wide by 7.5 blocks long. Most quilters don't want half a block in their quilt's design, so there are two choices — increase the number of blocks in the quilt's length to eight, or decrease that number to seven. After making this decision, multiply the two numbers to find the total number of blocks needed.

In this example, the quilter's preference is to go longer, so the number of blocks in the quilt's length is rounded up to eight. The finished quilt will be 6 blocks wide by eight blocks long, for a total of 48 blocks.

Students' Works

It is interesting to see how other quilters use simple Split Nine-Patch, Light Nine-Patch, and Dark Nine-Patch blocks to create their own designs. Since there are so many design possibilities, hundreds of quilts can be made without using the same design twice.

The quilts presented in this section were all created by quilters who took the author's class on this technique. They were encouraged to use their imaginations, and their likes and dislikes to create quilts reflecting their own personalities.

Barbara Kanta-Kinsey, Barbara Jo Fish, and Nancy Wasserman enjoy realistic quilts, so they used Nine-Patch blocks to create realistic wall-hangings. Sue Halsted and Gail Burrow love to appliqué. Their Nine-Patch quilts gave them a perfect spot to appliqué to their heart's content.

Marilyn Badger is an accomplished machine quilter. She enjoyed piecing the Nine-Patch blocks into an interesting pattern. Before quilting her quilt, she decided to experiment and added some threadwork designs. The result is an extraordinary quilt.

Ruth Spurlock found an interesting design option. She mixed smaller blocks and larger blocks to make a star within a star. Gale Davis discovered that Nine-Patch blocks in a Streak of Lightning setting created a perfect border for an unfinished project.

For those quilters who love geometric patterns, Nine-Patch blocks can be used to create wonderful designs. Beverly Fine twisted and turned her blocks until she came up with her delightful quilt.

Color can also create a unique quilt. Clear colors give a bold look, while muted colors give the quilt a misty quality. Johnnie McCallum's cheerful quilt reflects her love of bold, bright, clear colors. Shelia Woodard's quilt reflects her love of muted colors and is reminiscent of a Victorian garden.

As you look at these quilts, allow yourself to dream about the design possibilities for creating a quilt that reflects your personality.

Students' Works

◀ **MAY DAY**
46" x 46"
Marilyn Badger
Brookings, OR

Marilyn is a professional machine quilter. She was inspired by Libby Lehman's Threadplay technique and wanted to see if she could adapt the technique to a professional quilting machine. She mounted the quilt top on her machine and sewed the fancy threadwork. To quilt it, she then mounted it back onto the machine with the batting and backing. Note the original setting Marilyn used in her quilt and wide outer border.

MY BLUE AND YELLOW QUILT ▶
54" x 54"
Ruth Spurlock
Columbia, TN

Ruth based her original design on the traditional quilt block, Sawtooth Star. She wanted to create a blue and yellow quilt and found this technique perfect for her design. The smaller star within the larger star design creates interest and a sense of depth. The quilt is machine pieced and hand quilted. Metallic thread in the center of this beautiful quilt adds sparkle.

◀ **STAR IN MY PATH**
80" x 80"
Johnnie McCallum
Columbia, TN

Johnnie drew the inspiration for her scrap quilt from a Log Cabin design. She loves bright fabrics with clear colors; thus her quilt is bright, spirited, and cheerful. The quilt was machine pieced by Johnnie and machine quilted by Lin Hayden.

MAPLE LEAVES ▶
39" x 39"
Nancy Wasserman
Winchester, MA

Nancy's beautiful quilt was designed with a maple leaf in mind. As she looked through her scraps, she selected scraps with autumn-like colors. To echo the design, she repeated miniature maple leaves in the border, effectively using up almost all of her remaining scraps.

Students' Works

APRIL SHOWERS & MAY FLOWERS ▶
45" x 45"
Gail Burrow
Lewisburg, TN

Gail's lovely quilt combines a scrap quilt setting with appliqué. She designed the setting for her quilt by rotating the blocks on a flannel design wall. She wanted to leave a large area for appliqué in the center of the quilt and realized the scrap blocks would look like umbrellas if "handles" were added. She used the large area to hand appliqué flowers.

◀ P.T. 109
65" x 65"
Barbie Kanta-Kinsey
Columbia, TN

Barbie's goal was to make a quilt based on the traditional quilt block, Sailing Ship. Then, after the plane piloted by JFK Jr. went down, she decided to do a ship in his memory. JFK Jr. had named his sailboat PT 109 after his father's U.S. Navy boat, thus the name of this quilt. Barbie selected fabric prints that are reminders of JFK Jr. and his family. She machine pieced and machine quilted this beautiful quilt.

◀ DIAMOND IN A HEART
44" x 44"
Barbara Jo Fish
Linden, TN

This delightful quilt is an original design by Barbara Jo. She uses Split Nine-Patch, All-Light Nine-Patch, and All-Dark Nine-Patch blocks. This quilt is machine pieced and machine quilted.

GAITHER'S GARDEN ▶
81" x 81"
Shelia Woodard
Columbia, TN

Shelia's enticing quilt is reminiscent of a Victorian garden. She loves fabrics with muted, dusty colors and her quilt reflects her lovely fabric collection. Her quilt is machine pieced and machine quilted. The use of gray thread in the dark areas and a variegated thread in the light areas adds interest to her quilting.

Students' Works

PRIDE IN AMERICA ▶

64" x 81"
Gale S. Davis
Katy, TX

The flag medallion was an unfinished project and Gale used red and white split Nine-Patch blocks to create a striking border for her quilt. Gale machine pieced her quilt and the machine quilting was done by Chaille Voelkel of Katy, Texas. The center medallion of the quilt is a pattern, Forever Wave, from the book *Blessings* by Country Threads, 2345 Palm Avenue, Garner, IA 50438; (515) 923-3893.

◀ SCRAPS AND FLOWERS

42" x 42"
Sue Halsted
Columbia, TN

Sue's appealing quilt combines appliqué flowers and scrap blocks. She machine pieced and hand appliquéd her quilt. Robin Adams of Downer's Grove, Illinois, did the machine quilting. The appliqué flowers came from a pattern called Posy for Purse from the book *Willowood* by Jean Wells.

▲ BOW TO YOUR CORNER
63" x 100"
Beverly Fine
Lancaster, MA

Beverly made a Wedding Ring wallhanging using 9" blocks. But, after she finished the design, she decided to turn it on point and make it into a twin-sized bed quilt. While designing the borders, she added Split Nine-Patch blocks on the corners to create an interesting original design. Beverly's charming quilt is machine pieced and quilted by hand.

Chapter Five
Magic Results
From Simple Blocks

Scrap Quilts –
anything (and any fabric) goes!

These quilts are made from very scrappy blocks. Any dark fabric can be used on the dark side and any light fabric can be used on the light side. The color or pattern of the fabric does not matter, just as long as it is dark or light. Refer to Chapter 2, "Now You See It, Now You Don't," for more information on value and fabric selection.

Pg. 50

Pg. 54

Pg. 48

COMBING THROUGH YOUR SCRAPS – Karen Combs

Pg. 52

Pg. 56

Pg. 58

Pg. 60

Pg. 62

Controlled Colors

The first projects in this section use any color and any pattern in their blocks. As I pieced and sewed them, I wondered what would happen if I used only specific colors, or controlled the colors in the blocks.

While most quilts in this book use any color and fabric pattern in the blocks, the colors in scrap quilts can be controlled to achieve a different and unique effect.

The quilts on pages 64–70 are made by using one color on the dark side of a Split Nine-Patch block and a different color on the light side of the block. Controlling the colors gives an extra punch to value-based quilts – a punch you're sure to enjoy!

Pg. 70

Pg. 66

Pg. 68

Pg. 64

Miniature Quilts
From
Watercolor Squares

Pg. 74

Pg. 76

Pg. 72

Pg. 78

Many quilters have extra watercolor squares left over from making watercolor quilts. In some cases, they even have boxes of them! The scrappy quilts in this section, using Split Nine-Patch, All-Light or All-Dark Nine-Patch blocks, are perfect for those extra 2" squares. Since the color and pattern of the fabric don't matter, it is very easy and fun to use the 2" squares to make beautiful miniature quilts.

As with the larger versions of scrappy quilts, each Split Nine-Patch block will need a light side and a dark side.

These patterns use squares and triangles, and there is a quick trick that can be used to create triangles from the 2" squares. See page 31 for directions.

Pg. 80

FRIENDSHIP STAR
Wallhanging or Baby Quilt
Quilt size: 32" x 32"   Block size: 9"

MATERIALS

Assorted light and dark scraps
(see pages 16-17 for fabric yield)

Border: ⅓ yard medium value fabric

Batting: 35" square

Backing: 35" x 35"

Binding: ¼ yard

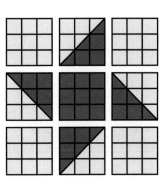
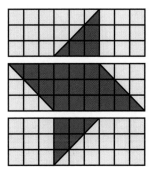

Figure 5-1.

CUTTING AND ASSEMBLY

1. From assorted light scraps, cut 48, 3½" squares and 12, 3½" triangles. (Rotary cut or use templates A and B, 9" finished block on page 24.)

2. From assorted dark scraps, cut 21, 3½" squares and 12, 3½" triangles. (Rotary cut or use templates A and B, 9" finished block on 24.)

3. Make 1 dark and 4 light Nine-Patch blocks as shown on page 22.

4. Make 4 Split Nine-Patch blocks as shown on page 21.

5. Arrange as shown in Figure 5-1 and sew blocks into rows. Press seams of alternating rows in opposite directions.

6. Sew the rows together (Figure 5-2), making sure to interlock seams as shown on page 21. Press.

7. From medium fabric, cut 2 border strips, 3" x 27" each, and sew them to either side of the quilt top. Cut 2 border strips 3" x 32", and sew to the top and bottom of the quilt top (Figure 5-3).

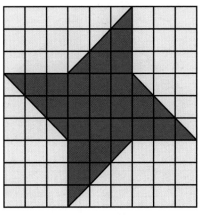

Figure 5-2.

QUILT FINISHING

1. Layer the quilt top with the square of batting and backing fabric. Baste.

2. Quilting suggestion: Outline quilt star. See Figure 5-3 or the photo.

3. Bind the edges of the quilt.

This traditional quilt block creates a wallhanging or a small baby quilt. FRIENDSHIP STAR quilt designed, machine pieced, and machine quilted by the author.

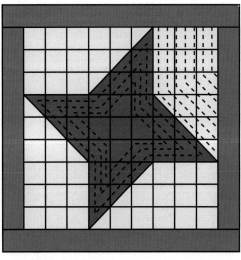

Figure 5-3.

WINDOW PANES
Wallhanging
Quilt size: 46" x 46"   Block size: 9"

MATERIALS

Assorted light and dark scraps
(see pages 16-17 for fabric yield)

Border: ½ yard dark value fabric

Dark and light sashing:

½ yard each fabric

Batting: 49" square

Backing: 49" x 49"

Binding: ¼ yard

CUTTING AND ASSEMBLY

1. From assorted light scraps, cut 48, 3½" squares and 48, 3½" triangles. (Rotary cut or use templates A and B, 9" finished block on page 24.)

2. From assorted dark scraps, cut 48, 3½" squares and 48, 3½" triangles. (Rotary cut or use templates A and B, 9" finished block on page 24.)

3. Make 16 Split Nine-Patch blocks (page 21).

4. From light sashing fabric, cut 8 strips 2" x 9½". Sew a sashing strip between 2 Split Nine-Patches as shown. Press seam toward sashing. Complete 8 units as shown in Figure 5-4.

5. From light sashing fabric, cut 4 strips 2" x 20". Sew a sashing strip between two units as shown in Figure 5-5. Press seam toward sashing. Make 4 units.

6. From dark sashing fabric, cut 2 strips 2" x 20". Sew a strip between units (Figure 5-6). Press seams toward sashing. Complete 2 units.

7. From dark sashing fabric, cut 2 strips, 2" x 41" each. Sew strip between units as shown in Figure 5-7. Press seams toward sashing.

8. From dark fabric, cut 2 border strips, 3" x 41" each, and sew to either side of the quilt top. Cut 2 border strips 3" x 46½" each, and sew to the top and bottom of the quilt top (Figure 5-8).

QUILT FINISHING

1. Layer the quilt top with batting and backing fabric. Baste.

2. Quilting suggestion: Stitch diagonally across the Split Nine-Patch blocks. See Figure 5-8 or the photo for details.

3. Bind the edges of the quilt.

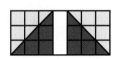
Figure 5-4.

Figure 5-5.

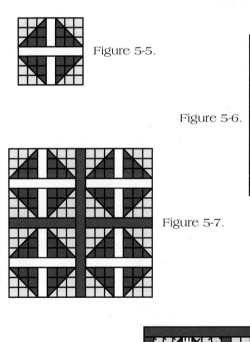
Figure 5-6.

Figure 5-7.

Figure 5-8.

The inspiration for this quilt came from the author's kitchen windows. She wondered what would happen if she separated Split Nine-Patch blocks by several sashes, much as the windows were separated by wood sashes. This quilt is the result of that "what if" question. WINDOW PANES quilt designed, machine pieced, and machine quilted by the author.

OFFSET SPIRAL
Throw or Wallhanging

Quilt size: 45" x 63"   Block size: 9"

MATERIALS

Assorted light and dark scraps
(see pages 16-17 for fabric yield)

Batting: 48" x 67" rectangle

Backing: 48" x 67"

Binding: ⅜ yard

CUTTING AND ASSEMBLY

1. From assorted light scraps, cut 105, 3½" squares and 105, 3½" triangles. (Rotary cut or use templates A and B, 9" finished block on page 24.)

2. From assorted dark scraps, cut 105, 3½" squares and 105, 3½" triangles. (Rotary cut or use templates A and B, 9" finished block on page 24.)

3. Make 35 Split Nine-Patch blocks as shown on page 21.

4. Arrange as shown in Figure 5-9 and sew blocks into rows. Press seams of alternating rows in opposite directions.

5. Sew the rows together, making sure to interlock seams as shown on page 21. Press.

QUILT FINISHING

1. Layer the quilt top with 48" x 67" rectangle of batting and 48" x 67" rectangle of backing fabric. Baste.

2. Quilting suggestion: Machine quilt using a stipple design over the surface of the quilt. Use light thread in the light areas and dark thread in the dark areas.

3. Bind the edges of the quilt.

Figure 5-9.

While rotating quilt blocks in the computer software, The Electric Quilt™, the author stumbled upon this offset spiral setting. It makes an interesting quilt for a throw or wallhanging! OFFSET SPIRAL quilt designed, machine pieced, and machine quilted by the author.

IN DEPTH
Throw or Wallhanging
Quilt size: 55" x 55"   Block size: 9"

MATERIALS

Assorted light and dark scraps
(see pages 16-17 for approximate yardage)

Side pieces:

2 light, 14" squares, cut in half diagonally, twice (see Figure 5-10)

Corner pieces:

2 light, 13⅜" squares, cut in half diagonally (see Figure 5-11)

Border: ⅝ yard dark value fabric

Batting: 58" square

Backing: 58" x 58"

Binding: ⅜ yard

CUTTING AND ASSEMBLY

1. From assorted light scraps, cut 72, 3½" squares and 72, 3½" triangles. (Rotary cut or use templates A and B, page 24.)

2. From assorted dark scraps, cut 72, 3½" squares and 72, 3½" triangles (Rotary cut or use templates A and B, page 24).

3. Make 24 Split Nine-Patch blocks.

4. Arrange as shown in Figure 5-12 and sew blocks into rows. Press seams of alternating rows in opposite directions.

5. Sew side pieces (cut from 14" squares) to the end of each row (Figure 5-13).

6. Sew rows together, making sure to interlock seams as shown on page 21. Press.

7. Sew corner pieces (cut from 13⅜" squares) to each corner (Figure 5-14).

8. From dark fabric, cut 2 border strips, 3½" x 50" each and sew to either side of the quilt top. Cut 2 border strips 3½" x 55" each and sew to the top and bottom of the quilt top (Figure 5-15).

QUILT FINISHING

1. Layer quilt; top, batting, and backing fabric. Baste.

2. Quilting suggestion: Machine quilt using a stipple stitch. Use a light thread in the light areas and a dark thread in the dark areas.

3. Bind the edges of the quilt.

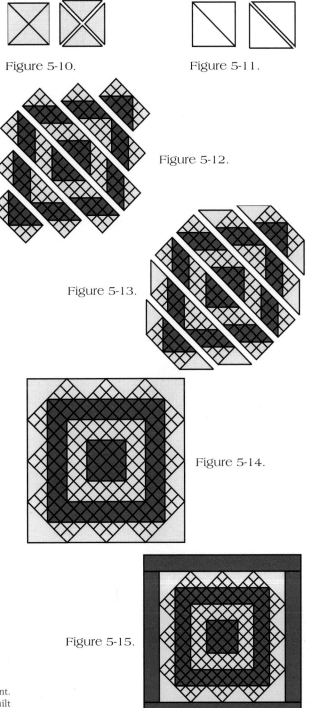

Figure 5-10.

Figure 5-11.

Figure 5-12.

Figure 5-13.

Figure 5-14.

Figure 5-15.

It's amazing what happens when you set Split Nine-Patch blocks on point. This quilt is an excellent size for a throw or wallhanging. IN DEPTH quilt designed, machine pieced, and machine quilted by the author.

COMBING THROUGH YOUR SCRAPS – Karen Combs

SUNRISE STAR
Throw or Wallhanging
Quilt size: 60" x 60"   Block size: 9"

MATERIALS

Assorted light and dark scraps
(see pages 16-17 for approximate yardage)

Border: ⅝ yard dark value fabric

Batting: 63" square

Backing: 63" x 63"

Binding: ⅜ yard

CUTTING AND ASSEMBLY

1. From assorted light scraps, cut 132, 3½" squares and 96, 3½" triangles. (Rotary cut or use templates A and B, 9" finished block on page 24.)

2. From assorted dark scraps, cut 96, 3½" squares and 96, 3½" triangles. (Rotary cut or use templates A and B, 9" finished block on page 24.)

3. Make 4 All-Light Nine-Patch blocks as shown on page 22.

4. Make 32 Split Nine-Patch blocks as shown on page 21.

5. Arrange as shown in Figure 5-16 and sew blocks into rows. Press seams of alternating rows in opposite directions.

6. Sew the rows together, making sure to interlock seams (page 21). Press.

7. From dark fabric, cut 2 border strips, 3½" x 54½" each, and sew them to either side of the quilt top. Cut 2 border strips 3½" x 60½" each, and sew to the top and bottom of the quilt top. (See Figure 5-17.)

QUILT FINISHING

1. Layer top, batting and backing fabric. Baste.

2. Quilting suggestion: Stipple in the light areas, using a light thread. In the dark areas, outline in ¼" to ½" repeats. See Figure 5-17.

3. Bind the edges of the quilt.

Figure 5-16.

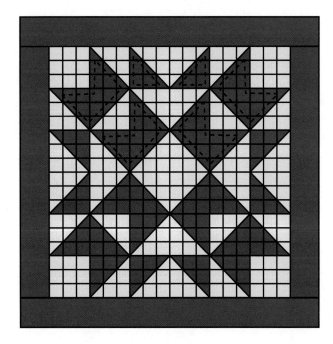

Figure 5-17.

The author loves stars, so she combined Split Nine-Patch blocks with All-Light Nine-Patch blocks to create this interesting and striking star quilt. An excellent size for a throw or wallhanging. SUNRISE STAR quilt designed, machine pieced, and machine quilted by the author.

SLANTED DIAMONDS
Wallhanging

Quilt size: 42" x 42"   Block size: 9"

MATERIALS

Assorted light and dark scraps
(see pages 16-17 for approximate yardage)

Border: ⅜ yard medium value fabric

Batting: 45" square

Backing: 45" x 45"

Binding: ¼ yard

CUTTING AND ASSEMBLY

1. From assorted light scraps, cut 48, 3½" squares and 48, 3½" triangles. (Rotary cut or use templates A and B, 9" finished block on page 24.)

2. From assorted dark scraps, cut 48, 3½" squares and 48, 3½" triangles. (Rotary cut or use templates A and B, 9" finished block on page 24.)

3. Make 16 Split Nine-Patch blocks.

4. Arrange as shown (Figure 5-18), sew blocks into rows. Press seams of alternating rows in opposite directions.

5. Sew the rows together, making sure to interlock seams (page 21). Press.

6. From medium fabric, cut 2 border strips, 3½" x 36½", and sew them to either side of the quilt top. Cut 2 border strips 3½" x 42", and sew them to the top and bottom of the quilt top. (See Figure 5-19.)

QUILT FINISHING

1. Layer the quilt top with a 45" square of batting, and a 45" square of backing fabric. Baste.

2. Quilting suggestion: In the dark and light areas, outline quilt the diamonds. See Figure 5-19 for details.

3. Bind the edges of the quilt.

This is an interesting design that can be used as a wallhanging or throw and can also be enlarged for a bed quilt. SLANTED DIAMONDS quilt designed, machine pieced, and machine quilted by the author.

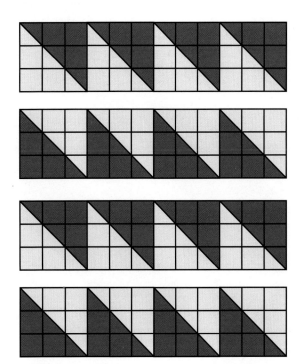

Figure 5-18.

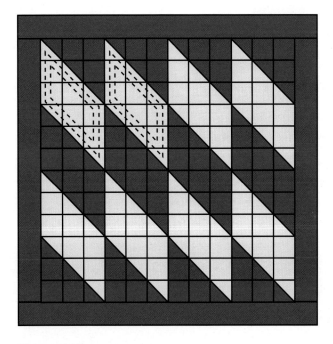

Figure 5-19.

COMBING THROUGH YOUR SCRAPS – Karen Combs

BARN RAISING

Throw or Wallhanging

Quilt size: 60" x 60"   Block size: 9"

MATERIALS

Assorted light and dark scraps
(see pages 16-17 for approximate yardage)

Border: ⅝ yard medium red fabric

Batting: 63" square

Backing: 63" x 63"

Binding: ⅜ yard

CUTTING AND ASSEMBLY

1. From assorted light scraps, cut 108, 3½" squares and 108, 3½" triangles. (Rotary cut or use templates A and B, 9" finished block on page 24.)

2. From assorted dark scraps, cut 108, 3½" squares and 108, 3½" triangles. (Rotary cut or use templates A and B, 9" finished block on page 24.)

3. Make 36 Split Nine-Patch blocks.

4. Arrange as shown and sew blocks into rows. Press seams of alternating rows in opposite directions.

5. Sew the rows together (Figure 5-20), making sure to interlock seams as shown on page 21. Press.

6. From medium red fabric, cut 2 border strips, 3½" x 54½" each, and sew them to either side of the quilt top. Cut 2 border strips 3½" x 60½" each, and sew them to the top and bottom of the quilt top (see Figure 5-21).

QUILT FINISHING

1. Layer the quilt top, batting, and backing. Baste.

2. Quilting suggestion: Stipple using light thread in the light areas and dark thread in the dark areas or outline quilt, as shown.

3. Bind the edges of the quilt.

Based on a Log Cabin setting, this quilt can be made as a wallhanging, a throw, or be increased to a bed size. BARN RAISING quilt designed, machine pieced, and machine quilted by the author.

Figure 5-20.

Figure 5-21.

Using light and dark batiks, this beautiful quilt has the appearance of stained glass. This quilt would fit a queen-sized bed; however, there is no pillow tuck an not much drop on the length of the quilt. If more drop is desired, enlarge the borders. Quilt designed, machine pieced, and machine quilted by author.

BEAUTIFUL BATIKS
Bed Quilt

Quilt size: 84" x 84"   Block size: 9"

MATERIALS

Assorted light and dark batik scraps
(see pages 16-17 for approximate yardage)

Tiny border:

¼ yard medium batik fabric

Border: ⅞ yard dark batik fabric

Batting: 90" x 90" rectangle

Backing: 90" x 90"

Binding: ½ yard

CUTTING AND ASSEMBLY

1. From assorted light batiks, cut 228, 3½" squares and 192, 3½" triangles. (Rotary cut or use templates A and B, 9" finished block on page 24.)

2. From assorted dark batiks, cut 192, 3½" squares and 192, 3½" triangles. (Rotary cut or use templates A and B, 9" finished block on page 24.)

3. Make 4 light Nine-Patch blocks.

4. Make 64 dark Split Nine-Patch blocks as shown on page 21.

5. Arrange and sew blocks into rows (Figure 5-30). Press seams of alternating rows in opposite directions.

6. Sew the rows together, making sure to interlock seams (page 21). Press.

7. Optional inner border – Cut ½" strip of fabric 81½" inches long. Fold in half, press flat. Layer between quilt top and outer border. Stitch together. Press flat against outer border.

8. From medium fabric, cut 4 border strips 3½" x 89" each, and attach to the quilt top, mitering corners (Figure 5-31).

QUILT FINISHING

1. Layer the top, batting, and backing. Baste.

2. Quilting suggestion: Stipple light areas and outline quilt dark areas.

3. Bind the edges of the quilt.

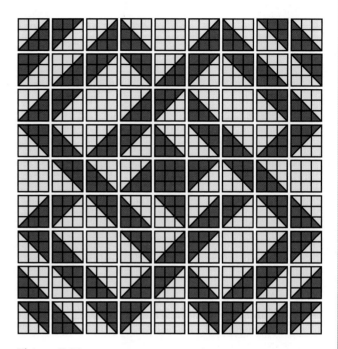

Figure 5-30.

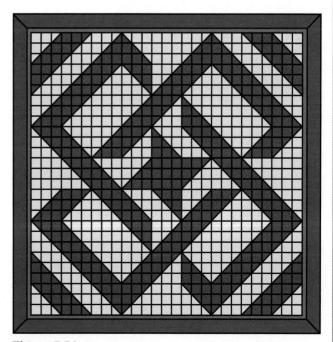

Figure 5-31.

HOUR GLASS
Wallhanging

Quilt size: 42" x 42"   Block size: 9"

MATERIALS

Assorted light green, dark teal, and dark purple scraps (see pages 16-17 for approx. yardage)

Border: ⅜ yard medium value fabric

Batting: 45" square from a crib-size batt

Backing: 45" x 45"

Binding: ¼ yard

CUTTING AND ASSEMBLY

1. From assorted light green scraps, cut 48, 3½" squares and 48, 3½" triangles. (Rotary cut or use templates A and B, 9" finished block on page 24.)

2. From assorted dark teal scraps, cut 24, 3½" squares and 24, 3½" triangles. (Rotary cut or use templates A and B, 9" finished block on page 24.)

3. From assorted dark purple scraps, cut 24, 3½" squares and 24, 3½" triangles. (Rotary cut or use templates A and B, 9" finished block on page 24.)

4. Make 8 light green and dark teal Split Nine-Patch blocks (page 21).

5. Make 8 light green and dark purple Split Nine-Patch blocks (page 21).

6. Arrange as shown in Figure 5-22 and sew blocks into rows. Press seams of alternating rows in opposite directions.

7. Sew rows together, making sure to interlock seams (page 21). Press.

8. From medium fabric, cut 2 border strips, 3½" x 36½" each, and sew to either side of the quilt top. Cut 2 border strips 3½" x 42½" each, and sew them to the top and bottom of the quilt top (see Figure 5-23).

This quilt is based the traditional Hour Glass quilt block. It works well as a scrappy quilt or as a controlled color wallhanging. The light side of the Split Nine-Patch block uses various light green fabrics. The dark side of the Split Nine-Patch block uses two colors, either dark teal or dark purple. Quilt designed, machine pieced, and machine quilted by author.

QUILT FINISHING

1. Layer quilt top, batting, backing fabric. Baste.

2. Quilting suggestion: Stipple light areas using a light thread. Outline quilt dark areas, using dark teal in the teal areas, and dark purple in the purple areas. See Figure 5-23 for quilting suggestions.

3. Bind the edges of the quilt.

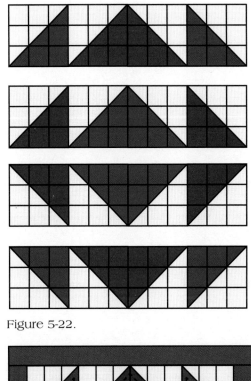

Figure 5-22.

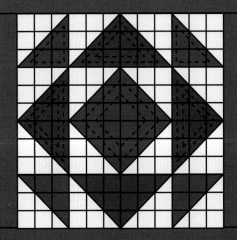

Figure 5-23.

COMBING THROUGH YOUR SCRAPS – Karen Combs

STAR PUZZLE
Wallhanging

Quilt size: 42" x 42"   Block size: 9"

MATERIALS

Assorted light green and dark red scraps
(see pages 16-17 for approximate yardage)

Border: ⅜ yard dark green value fabric

Batting: 45" square

Backing: 45" x 45"

Binding: ¼ yard

CUTTING AND ASSEMBLY

1. From assorted light green scraps, cut 48, 3½" squares and 48, 3½" triangles. (Rotary cut or use templates A and B, 9" finished block on page 24.)

2. From assorted dark red scraps, cut 48, 3½" squares and 48, 3½" triangles. (Rotary cut or use templates A and B, 9" finished block on page 24.)

3. Make 16 Split Nine-Patch blocks.

4. Arrange as shown (Figure 5-24),sew blocks into rows. Press seams of alternating rows in opposite directions.

5. Sew the rows together, making sure to interlock seams (page 21). Press.

6. From dark green fabric, cut 2 border strips, 3½" x 36½" each, and sew them to either side of the quilt top. Cut 2 border strips 3½" x 42½" each, and sew them to the top and bottom of the quilt top (see Figure 5-25).

QUILT FINISHING

1. Layer quilt top, batting, and backing. Baste.

2. Quilting suggestion: Outline quilt light areas using a light green thread. Outline quilt red areas using a dark red thread. See Figure 5-25 for quilting details.

3. Bind the edges of the quilt.

This quilt is based on the traditional quilt block Anna's Choice. The dark red and light apple green fabrics create a striking controlled scrap wallhanging. Quilt designed, machine pieced, and machine quilted by the author.

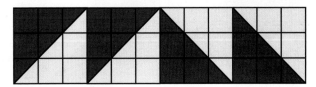

Figure 5-24.

Figure 5-25.

SUNSHINE AND SHADOW
Wallhanging

Quilt size: 51" x 51" Block size: 9"

MATERIALS

Assorted light blue and dark green scraps
(see page 16-17 for approximate yardage)

Light Blue Border:
  ⅓ yard light blue fabric

Dark Green Border:
  ½ yard dark green fabric

Batting: 53" square

Backing: 53" x 53"

Binding: ½ yard

CUTTING AND ASSEMBLY

1. From assorted light blue scraps, cut 75, 3½" squares and 75, 3½" triangles. (Rotary cut or use templates A and B, 9" finished block, page 24.)

2. From assorted dark green scraps, cut 75, 3½" squares and 75, 3½" triangles. (Rotary cut or use templates A and B, 9" finished block, page 24.)

3. Make 25 light blue and dark green Split Nine-Patch blocks (Page 21).

4. Arrange as shown (Figure 5-26), sew blocks into rows. Press seams of alternating rows in opposite directions.

5. Sew the rows together, making sure to interlock seams (page 21). Press.

6. From dark green fabric, cut 2 borders, each 3½" x 59" each, sew to left side, and bottom of quilt. Stop ¼" from corner, to allow for miter with light strips.

7. From light blue fabric, cut 2 border strips, 3½" x 59" each, sew to the top and right side of the quilt (Figure 5-27). Stop ¼" from the corner, miter remaining corners.

This design was inspired by a traditional Log Cabin setting and is made in controlled colors of light blue and dark green. This pattern can be made as a wallhanging or increased to bed size. Quilt designed, machine pieced, and machine quilted by the author.

QUILT FINISHING

1. Layer quilt top, batting, and backing. Baste.

2. Quilting suggestion: Outline quilt matching thread to the area quilted. See Figure 5-27 for quilting detail.

3. Bind the edges of the quilt.

Figure 5-26.

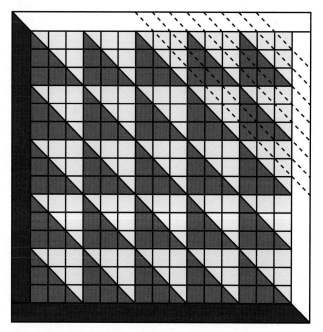

Figure 5-27.

The traditional quilt block, Flying Geese, inspired this original design with controlled colors. The light side of the Split Nine-Patch blocks use "vanilla" or off-white fabrics and the dark side of the Split Nine-Patch blocks is either dark purple or dark teal. Use this size as a wallhanging or throw, or increase it to a bed-sized quilt. Designed, machine pieced, and machine quilted by author.

Purple Mountain Majesty
Throw or Wallhanging
Quilt size: 52" x 52"   Block size: 9"

MATERIALS

Assorted off-white, dark purple and dark teal scraps (see pages 16-17 for approx. yardage)

1st Border: ⅜ dark teal fabric

2nd Border: ½ yard dark purple fabric

Binding: ⅜ yard

Batting: 56" square

Backing: 56" x 56"

CUTTING AND ASSEMBLY

1. From assorted off-white scraps, cut 75, 3½" squares and 75, 3½" triangles. (Rotary cut or use templates A and B, 9" finished square on page 24.)

2. From dark purple scraps, cut 45, 3½" squares and 45, 3½" triangles. (Rotary cut or use templates A and B, 9" finished square on page 24.)

3. From assorted dark teal scraps, cut 30, 3½" squares and 30, 3½" triangles. (Rotary cut or use templates A and B, 9" finished square on page 24.)

4. Make 15 off-white and dark purple Split Nine-Patch blocks (page 21).

5. Make 10 off-white and dark teal Split Nine-Patch blocks (page 21).

6. Arrange as shown and sew blocks into rows. Press seams of alternating rows in opposite directions.

7. Sew the rows together as shown in Figure 5-28, making sure to interlock seams as shown on page 21. Press.

8. From dark teal fabric, cut 2 border strips, 1½" x 45½" each and sew them to either side of the quilt top. Cut 2 border strips 1½" x 47½" each and sew them to the top and bottom of the quilt top.

9. From dark purple fabric, cut 2 border strips, 3½" x 47½" each, sew to either side of the quilt top. Cut 2 border strips 3½" x 53½" each and sew them

to the top and bottom of the quilt top (see Figure 5-29).

QUILT FINISHING

1. Layer the quilt top, batting, and backing fabric. Baste.

2. Quilting suggestion: Outline mountains matching thread to fabric. See Figure 5-29 for quilting details.

3. Bind the edges of the quilt.

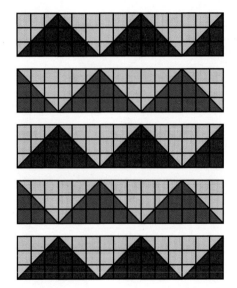

Figure 5-28.

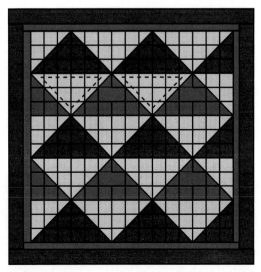

Figure 5-29.

COMBING THROUGH YOUR SCRAPS – Karen Combs

MINI SAMPLER
Miniature Quilt

Quilt size: 20" x 63"   **Block size: 4½"**

MATERIALS

Assorted light and dark 2" squares
(see pages 16-17 for approximate yardage)

1st Border: ¼ yard light fabric
2nd Border: ⅓ yard dark fabric
Batting: 24" x 66" rectangle
Backing: 24" x 66" rectangle
Binding: ¼ yard

CUTTING AND ASSEMBLY

1. Piece 144 triangle units as described on page 31. (Or use template B, 4½" finished block on page 24 to create 144 light and dark triangle units.)

2. From assorted light scraps, cut 144, 2" squares. (Rotary cut, use template A, 4½" finished block on page 24 or select from 2" watercolor squares.)

3. From assorted dark scraps, cut 144, 2" squares. (Rotary cut, use template A, 4½" finished block on page 24 or select from 2" watercolor squares.)

4. Make 48 Split Nine-Patch blocks.

5. Arrange blocks into designs as shown in Figure 5-38; sew blocks into rows.

6. Sew rows together, making sure to interlock seams (Page 21). Press.

1st Border

7. From dark fabric, cut 4 border strips, 1½" x 18½" each. Sew strips onto the top and bottom of quilt blocks as shown in Figure 5-39.

8. From same dark fabric, cut 2 border strips, 1½" x 58½" each. Sew them onto the right and left sides of the quilt (Figure 5-40).

2nd Border

9. From a medium value striped fabric, cut 2 border strips, 3" x 20½" each. Sew onto the right and left sides of the quilt.

10. From the same fabric, cut 2 border strips, 3" x 63½" each. Sew onto the right and left sides of the quilt. (Figure 5-41.)

QUILT FINISHING

1. Layer the quilt top, batting, and backing fabric. Baste.

2. Quilting suggestion: Outline quilt the blocks.

3. Bind the edges of the quilt.

Figure 5-38.

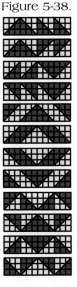

Figure 5-39.

Figure 5-40.

Figure 5-41.

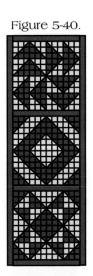

Three traditional quilt patterns – Variable Star, Dutchman's Puzzle, and Barn Raising – create a wonderful scrappy wall quilt. Quilt design, machine piecing and machine quilting by the author.

WEDDING RING
Miniature Quilt

Quilt size: 27" x 27"   Block size: 4½"

MATERIALS

Assorted light and dark 2" squares
(see pages 16-17 for approximate yardage)

Dark border: ¼ yard dark fabric

Batting: 30" square

Backing: 30" x 30"

Binding: ¼ yard

CUTTING AND ASSEMBLY

1. Piece 48 triangle units as described on page 31. (Or use template B, 4½" finished block on page 24 to create 48 light and dark triangle units.)

2. From assorted light scraps, cut 138, 2" squares. (Rotary cut, use template A, 4½" finished square on page 24 or select from 2" watercolor squares.)

3. From assorted dark scraps, cut 84, 2" squares. (Rotary cut, use template A, 4½" finished square on page 24 or select from 2" watercolor squares.)

4. Make 16 Split Nine-Patch blocks .

5. From assorted light squares make 5 All-Light Nine-Patch blocks.

6. From assorted dark squares make 4 All-Dark Nine-Patch blocks.

7. Arrange and sew blocks into rows (Figure 5-34). Press seams of alternating rows in opposite directions.

8. Sew rows together, making sure to interlock seams as shown on page 21. Press.

9. From dark fabric, cut 2 border strips, 2½" x 23" each. Sew them onto the right and left sides of the quilt.

10. From dark fabric, cut 2 border strips, 2½" x 27½" each, attach them to top and bottom of the quilt (Figure 5-35).

The traditional quilt pattern, Wedding Ring, was the inspiration for this striking miniature quilt. Quilt designed, machine pieced, and machine quilted by the author.

QUILT FINISHING

1. Layer quilt top, batting, and backing fabric. Baste.

2. Quilting suggestion: Outline with dark thread in the dark areas. Stipple in light areas, with light thread (See Figure 5-35).

3. Bind the edges of the quilt.

Figure 5-34.

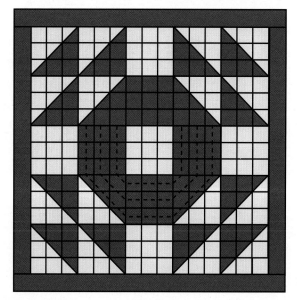

Figure 5-35.

KAREN'S STAR
Miniature Quilt

Quilt size: 33" x 33"   Block size: 4½"

MATERIALS

Assorted light and dark 2" squares
(see pages 16-17 for approximate yardage)

1st Border: ¼ yard light fabric
2nd border: ¼ yard dark fabric
Batting: 36" square
Backing: 36" x 36"
Binding: ¼ yard

CUTTING AND ASSEMBLY

1. Piece 108 triangle units as described on page 31. (Or use template B, 4½" finished block on page 24 to create 108 light and dark triangle units.)

2. From assorted light scraps, cut 108, 2" squares. (Rotary cut, use template A, 4½" finished block on page 24 or select from 2" watercolor squares.)

3. From assorted dark scraps, cut 108, 2" squares. (Rotary cut, use template A, 4½" finished block on page 24 or select from 2" watercolor squares.)

4. Make 36 Split Nine-Patch blocks.

5. Arrange and sew blocks into rows (Figure 5-36). Press seams of alternating rows in opposite directions.

6. Sew the rows together, making sure to interlock seams (page 21). Press.

7. From a bright fabric, cut 2 border strips, 1" x 27½" each. Sew onto the right and left sides of the quilt.

8. From a bright fabric, cut 2 border strips, each 1" x 28½". Sew onto the top and bottom sides of the quilt.

9. From dark fabric, cut 2 border strips, 3" x 28½"each. Sew them onto the right and left sides of the quilt.

10. From dark fabric, cut 2 border strips, 3" x 33½" each. Sew them onto the top and bottom of the quilt (Figure 5-37).

An original pattern that combines a Variable Star quilt block with a Log Cabin Barn Raising setting. Quilt design, machine piecing, and machine quilting by the author.

QUILT FINISHING

1. Layer the quilt top with a 36" square of batting and a 36" square of backing fabric. Baste.

2. Quilting suggestion: stipple quilt over the surface of the quilt.

3. Bind the edges of the quilt.

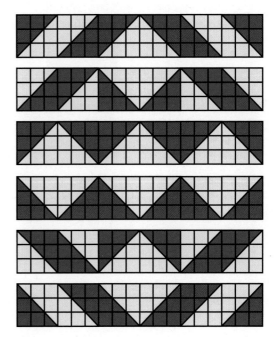

Figure 5-36.

Figure 5-37.

BROKEN DISHES
Miniature Quilt

Quilt size: 22" x 22"   Block size: 4½"

MATERIALS

Assorted light and dark 2" squares
(see pages 16-17 for approximate yardage)

Light border: ¼ yard light fabric
Dark border: ¼ yard dark fabric
Batting: 25" square
Backing: 25" x 25"
Binding: ¼ yard

CUTTING AND ASSEMBLY

1. Piece 48 triangle units as described on page 31. (Or use template B, 4½" finished block on page 24 to create 48 light and dark triangle units.)

2. From assorted light scraps, cut 48, 2" squares. (Rotary cut, use template A, 4½" finished block on page 24 or select from 2" watercolor squares.)

3. From assorted dark scraps, cut 48, 2" squares. (Rotary cut, use template A finished block on page 24 or select from 2" watercolor squares.)

4. Make 16 Split Nine-Patch blocks.

5. Referring to Figure 5-32 for arrangement, sew blocks into rows. Press seams of alternating rows in opposite directions.

6. Sew rows together, making sure to interlock seams (page 21). Press.

7. From dark fabric, cut 2 border strips, 2½" x 9½" each. From light fabric, cut 2 border strips, 2½" x 9½" each. Sew a light strip to a dark strip, sew to the right side of quilt. Make sure to align the border seam with the middle seam of the quilt. Repeat this step on the left side of the quilt.

8. From dark fabric, cut 2 border strips, 2½" x 11½" each. From light fabric,

cut 2 border strips, 2½" x 11½" each. Sew a light strip to a dark strip and sew them to the top of quilt (Figure 5-33). Be sure to align the border seam with the middle seam of the quilt. Repeat step on the bottom of the quilt.

QUILT FINISHING

1. Layer quilt top, batting, and backing fabric. Baste.

2. Quilting suggestion: See Figure 5-33 for quilting details.

3. Bind the edges of the quilt.

Figure 5-32.

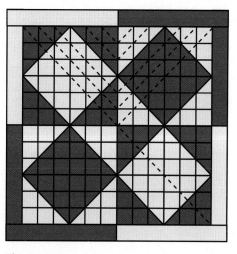

A traditional quilt pattern was the inspiration for this miniature scrappy quilt. The light and dark border treatment gives a unique look. Quilt designed, machine pieced, and machine quilted by the author.

Figure 5-33.

ROYAL STAR
Miniature Quilt
Quilt size: 41" x 41"   Block size: 4½"

MATERIALS

Assorted light and dark 2" squares
(see pages 16-17 for approximate yardage)

Border: ⅓ yard dark fabric

Batting: 44" square

Backing: 44" x 44"

Binding: ¼ yard

CUTTING AND ASSEMBLY

1. Piece 180 triangle units as described on page 31. (Or use template B, 4½" finished block on page 24 to create 180 light and dark triangle units.)

2. From assorted light scraps, cut 216, 2" squares. (Rotary cut, use template A, 4½" finished block on page 24 or select from 2" watercolor squares.)

3. From assorted dark scraps, cut 180, 2" squares. (Rotary cut, use template A, 4½" finished block on page 24 or select from 2" watercolor squares.)

4. Make 60 Split Nine-Patch blocks.

5. From assorted light squares, make 4 All-Light Nine-Patch blocks (page 22).

6. Arrange as shown in Figure 5-42 and sew blocks into rows. Press seams of alternating rows in opposite directions.

7. Sew rows together, making sure to interlock seams (Page 21). Press.

8. From dark fabric, cut 2 border strips, 3" x 36½" each. Sew them onto the top and bottom of the quilt.

9. From dark fabric, cut 2 border strips, 3" x 41½" each. Sew onto the right and left sides of the quilt (Figure 5-43).

This quilt was created using the computer program, Electric Quilt™. By rotating a Barn Raising setting placed around a Variable Star pattern, this design was born. The result is a striking quilt! Design, machine pieced, and machine quilted by the author.

QUILT FINISHING

1. Layer quilt top, batting, and backing fabric. Baste.

2. Quilting suggestion: Stipple quilt light areas with light thread. Outline quilt dark areas with dark thread. See photo for quilting detail.

3. Bind the edges of the quilt.

Figure 5-42.

Figure 5-43.

Chapter Six
Guild Fun &
Teaching Tips

IDEAS FOR GUILDS

Guilds often look for program ideas and community projects. The quilts in this book are easy to make and are perfect for guild projects. Use them as inspiration for programs or community projects.

SCRAP EXCHANGES

This is a fun and excellent way to provide a service for guild members.

Have each member bring as many 8" squares of light or dark valued fabric as they wish to exchange. Stipulate that the fabric squares be either very dark or very light in value. Or, for example, members could bring five dark blue floral squares, five light blue plaid squares, five dark red paisley squares, five light pink calico squares, and so on.

On tables, lay out the fabrics in light and dark piles, perhaps sorting them by color as well. Have each quilter note how many pieces of fabric they brought. Now the swap begins! A quilter who brings 20 squares can select the same number. The more each brings, the more they can swap, and the more variety each will have in their quilts.

From the traded squares, each person can cut squares and triangles to make scrap quilts.

GUILD BEES AND PROGRAMS

Many quilt guilds have quilt "bees," small groups that meet aside from the monthly meeting. Some bees meet weekly, some biweekly, and others, monthly. Many bees work on a selected idea such as appliqué, scrap quilts or other type of quilting.

This book contains excellent ideas for bees. During the bee meetings, quilters can exchange scraps, and piece blocks, and try out different settings. After making their quilts, the members of the bee could present a program to the guild showing the basic blocks and their resulting quilts.

COMMUNITY QUILTS

Many quilt guilds make quilts for different community charities, such as for women's shelters, nursing homes, and hospitals. Since quilt guilds want to make many quilts quickly, they look for quilt ideas that are fast and easy, yet have pleasing designs.

The quilts in this book can be made quickly and easily. Color and pattern of the fabric don't matter in these blocks – only value matters. Quilters can make blocks at home using their own fabrics and when the blocks are sewn into a quilt, they will all work together. As long as the values are correct, it does not matter what fabrics have been used.

MAKE QUILTS AS A GROUP

At the guild meeting to begin the project, the program chairman should show the basic Nine-Patch blocks and display a simple quilt using these blocks. This is the time to demonstrate the types of fabrics to use and piecing techniques.

During the next few months, members can work on their Nine-Patch blocks at home. If needed, a scrap exchange can be planned.

Set aside a guild meeting to set the blocks together. Do this in an assembly-line fashion with one group squaring up blocks, a group pinning, another group sewing blocks together, and yet another group pressing. Since there are so many designs, the hardest part may be selecting which ones to do!

It is fun to see these quilt tops go together and many can be sewn during a guild meeting. After making the tops, members can take them home for quilting and binding.

IDEAS FOR QUILT TEACHERS

The ideas and quilts in this book are also ideal for multi-week classes. Below you will find class descriptions, class outlines, supply lists, and other ideas to help make a class successful.

PROMOTING THE CLASS

The most valuable promotion for a class held in a quilt shop is a good sample of a class project. Make sure the sample is attractive and well-constructed. It should be displayed in a highly-visible area, not hung in a dark corner. Some shops find it helpful to place a sign on the sample, listing times, dates, and cost of the class.

Another valuable promotional tool is a newsletter or flyer describing the class. Many shops mail a quarterly newsletter listing classes, sales, interesting products, and other information. Use the class description below to increase interest in the class.

CLASS DESCRIPTION (for shop newsletter)

Put your fabric stash to good use. Make a scrap quilt using quick, template-free methods. Learn to feel comfortable putting many fabrics together, distinguishing "value," and making many different scrap wallhangings or quilts.

You will work on a quilt in class using shared fabrics from your classmates. This is a great place to use "ugly" fabrics – they look great in this quilt! Bring extra fabric to share.

CLASS GOALS

During the class, students will

- learn how to combine different types of fabrics.
- learn to properly rotary cut squares and triangles.
- learn to sew with an accurate ¼" seam allowance.
- learn to correctly match seams.
- learn to machine chain piece.
- understand the numerous design possibilities with the basic blocks.
- finish a wallhanging in class or finish a full-sized quilt at home.
- plan quilting design and understand how to bind a quilt.

CLASS SIZE

Consider the size of the classroom and the instructor's teaching experience before deciding how many students to accept into a class. Twenty students is probably the largest class size to consider.

CLASS LENGTH

These scrap quilt ideas are suitable for a class that meets once a week for four weeks, or for a one-time, all-day workshop. For an all-day, 6-hour workshop, it is important to meet with students before the class. Help them buy fabric, show them a few samples of the blocks, and demonstrate how to rotary cut squares and triangles. The students will need to precut their squares and triangles before class.

CLASSROOM SETUP

The classroom setup will depend on the workshop's location and available space. Keep this in mind while reading through the information below. With a small room, it may be necessary to have more students at each table or fewer students in a class.

I suggest no more than two students to a table. Each student will need room for a sewing machine, cutting surface, and design surface.

Each student should have access to their own design wall. Their design wall – a piece of flannel or even batting – can be taped to the wall and taken home at the end of each class.

Four (or fewer) students to each ironing surface is ideal. Be careful, irons use a great deal of electricity. If you are in an old building, you could blow a fuse. Check this out before scheduling the class. Also make sure there are adequate outlets. If not, you may need to provide power strips and extension cords.

SUPPLY LIST

A supply list can be given to students when they sign up for the class, or the list can be printed in a newsletter or flyer.

In order not to violate copyright laws, do not make photocopies of the illustrations or quilt patterns from this book (or any other). Rather, require that each student have their own book. They can purchase a copy before the class, or the cost of the book can be added to the workshop fee and the books distributed to students when they sign up for the class.

Supply list for students

____*Combing Through Your Scraps* book
____rotary cutter & cutting mat
____rotary rulers (6" x 12" and 6" x 6")
____straight pins
____sewing machine threaded with off-white or light gray thread
____scissors
____seam ripper
____1 yard of flannel for a design wall
   (leftover batting will work in a pinch)
____tape to hang design wall
____Fabrics: Fat quarters of light and dark

fabrics. Bring all colors but make sure to include some light yellows, dark reds and some "uglies" in the selection. The more fabrics, the better trading will be encouraged during class. This is a wonderful project on which to use your stash. Since the design and color of the fabric do not matter, bring fabrics you would like to use up.

If you have boxes and boxes of 2" watercolor squares, you can use them instead of larger patches. Your wallhanging will be smaller, but it will be beautiful!

Supply list for the teacher

____rotary cutter & cutting mat
____rotary rulers (6" x 6" and 6" x 12")
____handouts & samples
____red and green value finder tool for each student (to make value finder tools, see page 11).
____*Combing Through Your Scraps* book
____sewing machine threaded with neutral thread
____basic sewing supplies

SUGGESTIONS FOR TEACHERS

- Bring a nametag for each student.
- Arrive at least 40 minutes early to set up the classroom. Many students arrive early, and it's a good idea to have the classroom ready.
- Encourage questions. Remember, there are NO dumb questions.
- Be helpful to each student and, if possible, give equal time to each one.
- Give positive and constructive criticism. Gently suggest how to correct mistakes and always point out the positive first.
- Keep focused on the class. This is not the time for the instructor to tell students about personal problems.
- Students are taking the class because they love quilting or want to learn a new technique. If a student starts talking about personal issues, gently guide the class back to the fun of quilting.

• The instructor should have a positive attitude and speak in a cheerful, upbeat manner. They should be knowledgeable about their subjects and give clear instructions. An instructor should NEVER teach a technique they have not tried. Reading about a technique is not a substitute for doing the technique. Instructors should also have a passion for quilting and share it with students.

WEEKLY CLASS FORMAT

SESSION ONE

Demonstrate how to rotary cut squares and triangles. This is a good time to teach students the "magic" numbers for rotary cutting squares and triangles.

"Magic" Numbers

Example
3" finished

+ ½" = 3½"
cutting measurement

Squares: Add ½" to the desired finished size.

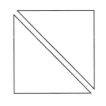

Example
3" finished

+ ⅞" = 3⅞"
cutting measurement

Triangles: Add ⅞" to the desired finished size.

Students should be shown how to "stack" fat quarters to quickly cut out shapes. Help them determine what size quilt they would like to make. For more information, see page 35, "What Size Should I Make My Quilt?"

Homework: Students should cut out enough squares and triangles to make their quilt.

ROTARY SAFETY

This class emphasizes quick piecing using the rotary cutter. This handy tool has a sharp blade that can easily cut or scratch fingers if improper safety techniques are used. Here are some suggestions for the classroom:

• Be prepared by knowing the location of first-aid supplies.
• Carry a box of adhesive bandages with teaching supplies.
• Emphasize the proper use of rotary cutters and safety techniques before students use cutters.
• Demonstrate proper cutting procedures.
• Caution students to close the guard on the rotary cutter when it is not in their hand.
• Be alert for the beginning student who has never used a rotary cutter.
• Spend extra time with that student to help develop proper cutting techniques.

SESSION TWO

Show the different types of Nine-Patch blocks. Lay out a block and demonstrate how to distinguish value using the value tools. Demonstrate how to sew a block. Show chain piecing, how to match seams, and how to press. Have students begin sewing blocks. Check their work.

Homework: Have students make blocks at home.

SESSION THREE

Show different quilt designs. Have students pick out a design, and sew rows together.

Homework: Have students finish sewing rows together.

SESSION FOUR

Demonstrate different border and quilting options. Add borders onto quilt. Suggest different quilting options. Show students how to bind a quilt. A demonstration can be done on a small sample.

Bibliography

Beyer, Jinny, *Quilter's Album of Blocks and Borders*, EPM Publications, 1980.

Brackman, Barbara, *Encyclopedia of Pieced Quilt Patterns*, American Quilter's Society, 1993.

Blockbase™ Version 1.0, The Electric Quilt Co., 1991 – 1995.

Electric Quilt™ Version 3.0, The Electric Quilt Col., 1991 – 1996.

Hopkins, Judy, *Around the Block*, That Patchwork Place, 1994.

Lehman, Libby, *Threadplay*, That Patchwork Place, 1997.

Liby, Shirley, *Exploring Four Patch*, Shirley Liby, 1988.

Liby, Shirley, *Designing with Nine Patch*, Shirley Liby, 1989.

Miller, Phyllis D., *Encyclopedia of Designs for Quilting*, American Quilter's Society, 1996.

Noble, Maurine, *Machine Quilting Made Easy!*, That Patchwork Place, 1994.

Quilt-Pro™ Version 2.0, Quilt-Pro Systems, 1994 – 1995.

Rehmel, Judy, *The Quilt I.D. Book*, Prentice Hall Press, 1986.

Sources

Fabric swatches packets
Benartex, Inc.
1460 Broadway
8th Floor
New York, NY 10036
http://www.benartex.com

The Cotton Club
P.O. Box 2263
Boise, ID 83701
http://www.cottonclub.com

Hancock's of Paducah
3841 Hinkleville Road
Paducah, KY 42001
http://www.Hancocks-Paducah.com

Keepsake Quilting
Route 25B
P.O. Box 1618
Centre Harbor, NH 03226-1618
http://wwwkeepsakequilting.com

¼" seam sewing machine foot
Little Foot® Ltd.
798 Terrace Avenue
P. O. Box 1027
Chama, NM 87520
(800) 597-7075
http://www.littlefoot.net

Sewing machine needles and thread
Clotilde, Inc.
B3000
Louisiana, MO 63353-3000

Web of Thread
1410 Broadway
Paducah, KY 42001
(800) 955-8185
http://www.webofthread.com

Fabric dye fixative
Retayne™
Dharma Trading Co.
P.O. Box 150916
San Rafael, CA 94915
(800) 542-5227
http://www.dharmatrading.com

Machine quilters
Marilyn Badger
15957 Highway 101 South, Suite 3
Harbor, OR 97415
Mbadge@harborside.com

Barbie Kanta-Kinsey
2514 Sowell Mill Pike
Columbia, TN 38401-7446
(931) 381-4769
Piececorps@juno.com

About the Author

Karen Combs is an internationally known quilter, teacher, author, and designer, nominated by students for Quilt Teacher of the Year in 1995 and 2000.

Teaching since 1989, she is in high demand as an instructor who encourages her students, makes learning fun, and makes the complex easy to understand!

A confessed fabricholic, Karen loves collecting fabrics. With her own fabric stash out of control, she created an easy way to use any light or dark fabric to create beautiful scrap quilts. She shares this technique in *Combing Through Your Scraps*.

Fascinated with optical illusions in quilts, Karen teaches on the subject in many of her workshops. She is the author of *Optical Illusions for Quilters* and the co-author of *3-D Fun with Pandora's Box*.

Karen lives in the rolling hills of middle Tennessee with her husband Rick, daughter Angela (when she is home from college), son Josh, and a cute Shih Tzu named Cocoa.

To learn more about Karen's quilts or classes, visit her website at http://www.karencombs.com.

Photo by
Debbie Gaskill Photography

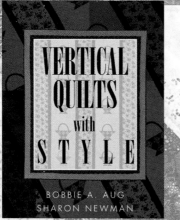
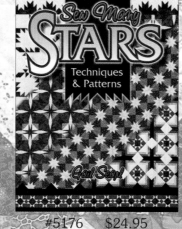
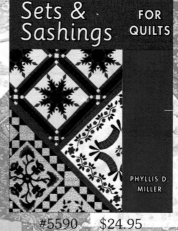